PR IN PRACTICE SERIES

Public Relations

A practical guide to the basics

Philip Henslowe

Second Edition

the Institute *of* Public Relations

KOGAN
PAGE

London and Sterling, VA

Dedicated to my wife, Elizabeth

First published in 1999
Reprinted 2001, 2002
Second edition 2003

120 Pentonville Road
London N1 9JN
UK

22883 Quicksilver Drive
Sterling VA 20166-2012
USA

www.kogan-page.co.uk

British Library Cataloguing in Publication Data

A CIP record for this book is available from the British Library.

ISBN: 0 7494 4072 4

Library of Congress Cataloging-in-Publication Data

Henslowe, Philip, 1934-
    Public relations : a practical guide to the basics / Philip
Henslowe.--2nd ed.
        p. cm.
Includes bibliographical references and index.
        ISBN 0-7494-4072-4
        1. Public relations--Handbooks, manuals. etc. 2. Public
relations--Great Britain--Handbooks, manuals, etc. I. Title.
    HD59.H443 2003
    659.2--dc22

2003015170

Typeset by JS Typesetting Ltd, Wellingborough, Northants
Printed and bound in Great Britain by Clays Ltd, St Ives plc

Contents

Foreword

So, you are absolutely new to your first job and it has something to do with public relations. Or maybe you work in an organization that hasn't really done public relations and you've been asked to get on with it. The problem is, you're not sure what to do.

Perhaps you work for a charity or voluntary organization that cannot afford a public relations professional and you need to become familiar with what's involved. This book is for you. Philip Henslowe gives a basic introduction to public relations and introduces some very useful 'How tos'. This isn't a detailed guide, neither does it pretend to give any more than an overview, but as an 'in' to the public relations discipline, it gives a solid base to work from.

Philip provides the legal and ethical framework of public relations practice and then goes on to indicate how those involved in public relations work with other fellow professionals who act as suppliers, photographers, printers, designers and the media (including video makers). He then goes on to describe how to organize exhibitions, displays and functions and includes a useful section on Royal visits. One of the key tasks of practitioners is of writing. Again, Philip takes the practical approach to business writing, copy and feature writing and devotes a whole section to this skill. There is also useful guidance on sponsorship, crisis management, working with the media and on planning and evaluating campaigns.

What the book does not do is cover all the functional areas of public relations such as internal communications, marketing communications, public affairs and the like. There are plenty of books around that do this job. Philip is aiming to provide the potential practitioner with a raft of knowledge and skills that underpin the range of public relations activity.

Thus the book fulfils its brief. It is a basic guide for all who wish to work in the public relations area – whatever their future specialism may be.

Anne Gregory
Series Editor

Preface

Public relations is not, nor should it be, a 'stand-alone' profession, in isolation from the rest of the business world. It is all about communication. Communication, and thus public relations, is playing an increasingly important role in the changing world today, in everyday life, in business, politics and world affairs. It is associated and connected, both directly and indirectly, to commerce and business, to professions and occupations, often encompassing many different and sometimes apparently unrelated areas – marketing, advertising, market research, internal and external communication both in the public and private sectors, to name but a few.

Those who work in public relations today are expected to be aware, at the very least, of those other areas on which their work impinges. Public relations is often the way forward, the link that enables all these areas to work together – to communicate with each other.

It does not necessarily mean having to become an expert in those areas concerned. Nevertheless, a good working knowledge of them is essential in order to recognize and appreciate the special problems, specialist skills and knowledge that are required in the different disciplines in the workplace.

This book has been written not only for those already working in public relations, but also for those who are coming into the communication industry. Since the first edition of this book was written much has changed, and this new edition brings up to date information on a number of different areas of work. However, it is not, nor is it intended to be, encyclopaedic in its content, but rather to be used as a ready reference. It gives the reader an overview of most of the main areas of work, with some detail where appropriate, or refers the reader to more detailed and available works of reference elsewhere.

Therefore, I hope that this revised edition will continue to be a useful guide for those working in, or wanting to enter, the world of public relations.

Acknowledgements

When I wrote the first edition of this book, I drew to a great extent on both my own experience and that of others, together with the many published works in this field, and was most grateful then for the help and assistance I obtained from all these sources. Particularly, I was indebted to the late Professor Sam Black and Frank Jefkins, who were partly the inspiration behind writing it and to many others. Amongst them were Professor Anne Gregory, Neil King, The Bournville Village Trust, Ikon Design Limited for the use of some of their material and Bert Hackett (*Gemini* of the Birmingham Post) for his cartoons.

For this, the second edition, my particular thanks must go to Dr Sheila Lodge, Head of School of Communication Arts at Napier University, Edinburgh, and to Myra Tait in the School office, for their help in setting up all the various meetings for me. To Mairi Sutherland, Derek Allan, Myrna MacLeod, Brenda Munro and Louise Welsh, also at Napier University, for all their support, time, help and advice, especially on some of the more technical aspects, ensuring that they are accurate and up to date – thank you. My grateful appreciation also to Bernard Harrison for putting me right on the photographic side, and to Debra Levy at the Press Association for all her time and help.

For more detailed treatment of some areas of public relations work, refer to further reading on page 107.

1

Communication and the roles of public relations

INTRODUCTION

This chapter is intended to remind the reader of a few basic facts about communication and public relations generally, how they relate and their significance and importance in our daily lives and in our work.

Communication and public relations are inextricably linked to each other and play an important part in a wide variety of ways throughout our lives. Increasingly, organizations are now acknowledging that a communications professional is now a necessary appointment within its structure.

However, the term 'public relations' is often either misunderstood or deliberately misinterpreted, so that it is used in a pejorative way, associating it with propaganda, 'economy of the truth' or evasion. Different people therefore have different perceptions of public relations. Those who work in the industry are often viewed with suspicion by those who work in the media, who misunderstand its roles. There are some individuals, often highly placed in industry, who expect public relations to be used as a tool for whitewashing reputations, or for covering up acts of ineptitude or dishonesty.

Public relations is a complex profession, an emerging industry that is at the heart of all communication. It is also a powerful one that is growing and, to an extent, gaining respect throughout the world today. It covers a wide spectrum of both specialist and general areas of work and offers a wide range of options with many opportunities for those who wish to specialize in it. The skills that are needed to become a specialist in communication are of the highest order and are transferable.

There are now a number of opportunities to study and gain professional qualifications through exams, degree programmes and short courses in public relations for those wishing to further their career in this field.

COMMUNICATION

In everyday life

Communication, in one form or another, plays a significant part in our daily lives in a wide variety of ways, throughout our life. It is always there. We use it all the time, often without realizing, depending on our particular needs or desires at that moment.

Actions can often speak louder than words. We can communicate by merely looking, by speaking, by posture, or by our actions. If used properly, communication can be used to inform, educate, reassure, evoke sympathy, arouse interest in, or acceptance of, situations as and when they occur. For example, when shopping, your manner towards sales assistants and the way they respond to you can make the difference between a sale or not. Going for an interview, the first and most important impression that you give is made on entering the interview room, through how you look, how you dress, how you speak, your manner and your attitude. All these are different forms of communication; some are silent, some are not.

It must also always be remembered that communication is a two-way process. Messages and information received are just as important as those that are sent. The same applies to public relations. It is all about communicating with others, whether by the written word, by the spoken word, or by visual or some other means.

In the workplace

It is now universally acknowledged that communication, through the medium of public relations, has an essential role to play in all aspects of business, in industry, commerce, in public services and in government; the latter both nationally and internationally, as witnessed, for example, by the enormous amount of interest generated by the ongoing Middle East crises.

In the last decade, there has been a tremendous upsurge in the diverse use of public relations in the workplace generally. In this context, public relations is concerned with the different ways of establishing and maintaining a sound two-way communication between the organization and everyone with whom it has any form of contact. This will include, among others, its stakeholders, the various publics with whom it deals, its workforce and, of course, the media.

In different forms, public relations can affect all shapes and sizes of organizations, whether large or small, private or public, commercial or in the private sector. Even the Royal Family has been shown not to be immune to it, as was shown by both the Burrell trial and other subsequent events, all of them highlighted by the media.

Communication, in one form or another, whether internal or external, is something that cannot be avoided or ignored by any organization. To do so will not only be disastrous for it in the short term, but can also seriously damage its reputation in the longer term.

Government at all levels, therefore, now has to be much more accountable; not only to be seen to communicate with all the various 'publics' much more readily and more often, but to do so effectively. In each central government department today, for instance, there are established press and public relations offices with public relations staff, press officers and expert advisers available. Their task is to inform, advise and brief their ministers and their other publics regarding any new governmental or departmental policies, changes, or developments, and to provide other relevant information, as and when it occurs. They also have to update the media, on a regular basis, through press conferences and other forms of releases. Similarly, today, in the public services and in local government, at both county and at district levels, public relations and press offices are now part of the normal establishment.

There is a growing awareness that all organizations, large and small, whether private companies or public corporations, now have to be much more accountable and communicate with all their various publics more readily, and more frequently than ever before. They, too, have had to accept that the media, and their publics generally, are much more questioning now than in the past.

CORPORATE COMMUNICATION

Corporate communication, in one form or another, is no longer a luxury but a necessity, because both the media and the public are today much more questioning than in the past. Therefore, today, openness and public accountability have become essential.

The failure to communicate openly can lead to a loss of credibility on world markets, often followed by financial losses due to lost orders, and the inevitable 'knock-on' effect that all this generates. It often results in manufacturing facilities and factories having to close, creating considerable unemployment, both local and regional, with all that stems from that. There have been many examples of this in recent years, both in the UK and elsewhere.

The lack of openness, accountability and communication when it was most needed is evidenced by UK Government's departmental crises arising from the Foot and Mouth epidemic and the state of the transport systems in this country. The Enron scandal in the United States and its implications for UK firms and operations, the problems faced by some of our major financial institutions in the City and in the insurance industry recently, all show how important accountability can be.

CORPORATE SOCIAL RESPONSIBILITY

Another more recent area in which communication through public relations has a key role concerns corporate social responsibility, or CSR, as it is more commonly known. This covers all aspects of an organization and its work and could be said to be the conscience of that organization. CSR embraces all the corporate policies, both internal and external, their operation, and corporate responsibility to stakeholders, ethical investment, work practices and trading generally.

With the increasing uncertainty in the international commercial and industrial scene at present, coupled with the political situations worldwide and external pressures being put on organizations, CSR is fast becoming a major factor in many organizations today.

In the voluntary sector

These same principles of communication also apply to other types of organizations, in the private, voluntary, charitable and non-charitable sectors, both large and small. The marked increase both in the number and the activities of charitably based organizations in this country has led to a greater need for public awareness and appreciation of their work both nationally and internationally.

This has led to the introduction of considerable communication activity and the upsurge in a variety of public relations operations in this sector. In terms of the latter, the main role of public relations staff is to inform and educate both the public and the media, making them aware of the organizations concerned, explaining the nature of their work and their activities generally. Most voluntary bodies, charities and housing associations in the UK now have full-time public affairs, or public relations, staff within their organization; something that was relatively uncommon until a few years ago, with very few exceptions.

An indication of how important and significant the growth in this sector is considered to be is reflected by the relaunch of the weekly publication *Third Sector*. It covers all aspects of the communication policies, and therefore the public relations work, being carried out in this rapidly expanding sector.

In education

Similarly, universities and most colleges now consider communication to be sufficiently important for them to have an internal public relations office, or corporate affairs department; some also having additional external resources available.

Many of the larger schools, both in the independent and private sectors, now have a member of staff who, in addition to his or her normal role, eg as bursar, is also responsible for dealing with external communication of the school's activities. This can be particularly important where the school or college concerned may have a high profile due to particular circumstances.

PUBLICITY

The use of publicity as a form of communication, particularly in promoting celebrities either as individuals or as groups, has become fashionable in certain elements of our society today and generates a great deal of media interest. The aim is to give the subject, or subjects, the maximum amount of coverage in whatever way possible.

It is usually generated by 'publicists' and 'spin doctors', often with manipulation of the media involved. However, although publicity often claims to be public relations, it is not public relations in its true sense, and should not be confused with it.

IMAGES

An important part of public relations work is the image. What is meant by image? It can be defined as being: 'The impression gained according to the level of knowledge and understanding of facts (about people, products or situations).' Wrong or incomplete information will give a wrong image. For example, people often refer to 'India', meaning the whole sub-continent, whereas in fact India is only part of it, together with Pakistan and Bangladesh, both independent states in their own right.

Different images

There are several different sorts of image, all of which have roles for public relations:

● *the mirror image* – what we think we look like – often an illusion due to wishful thinking. For example, your image that you see in the mirror can look quite different to a photograph of yourself.

- *the current image* – what people outside think of an organization, or a person. Often this image is distorted; usually due to mis-understanding, a lack of knowledge about the individual or the organization, or even to hostility. However, the CSR policy of an organization can help to turn that current image to its advantage. Similarly, in equivalent terms, the current image of an individual can likewise be altered.
- *the corporate image* – the image of the organization. This is very important in terms of public relations and also as part of the CSR of that organization. Made up of many facts, such as its history, reputation, stability, financial success, etc, the corporate image, or how an organization presents itself to the outside world, is a vital part of its CSR.
- *the multiple image* – sometimes organizations have different divisions, with each having its own, quite separate corporate identity, or image. This can be confusing to the public, but can be overcome by using symbols, badges or other means to provide an identifiable 'group' image.

If public relations is not used to correct possible misconceptions and illusions given out by these different images they can have a damaging effect on the reputation of the organization concerned by confusing its public.

KNOWLEDGE AND UNDERSTANDING

Public relations has a key role to play in helping to inform both its own public and other, far wider ones, by providing information in a factual, easily understood format, so that ignorance of an organization, a product or a place can be overcome through knowledge and understanding.

A good example of this has been the increasing use of public relations by many charities, housing associations and other voluntary bodies in recent years, both to inform the media and the public, and to explain the nature of their work and their activities generally. This they have done very successfully.

INTEREST

Public relations also has a role to play in generating public interest in a particular situation, or set of circumstances, that may be having a major effect on an organization or group of people. Using public relations methods and techniques in this instance can be very effective.

ACCEPTANCE

People may be hostile to a situation because they simply do not understand what is happening, or why. Once they do understand, they will often much more readily accept it. Public relations has a clear role to play in explaining the particular situation or circumstances clearly, so that the ignorance, and even hostility, surrounding it can be turned into understanding and acceptance.

SYMPATHY

The role here for public relations is to promote understanding and knowledge of the facts about a set of circumstances or a situation in such a way as to gain sympathy for it. Clearly presented, unbiased information can often be the way to do this.

> Poor images come from ignorance, prejudice, hostility and apathy. Public relations can convert these into knowledge and understanding, acceptance and interest.

2

External public relations sources

INTRODUCTION

Public relations work is normally carried out either by the in-house resource of an organization or through some form of external resource, usually a public relations consultancy. On occasions, however, it can be a mix of both methods. This chapter looks in outline at some of the external resources that are available for public relations work.

CONSULTANCIES

A consultancy is not an agency, although the latter term is often used, misleadingly, when describing a consultancy. For example, a management consultancy is different from a management agency, in that the former offers a whole range of consultancy services, while the latter works on commission from employers.

Similarly, advertising agencies are 'agents' of the media, from whom they gain much of their income by commission on space and air-time. They get accredited or recognized by media owners' organizations (eg The National Press Agency, or the Independent Television Contractors Association). They are a sort of 'commission agent', unlike public relations consultancies, whose income comes from fees based on expertise, experience and the number of hours worked on a particular client's account.

WHY USE A CONSULTANCY?

Public relations consultancies are usually employed for the following reasons:

- The organization concerned is not big enough, financially or otherwise, to justify its own PR department.
- Company policy lays down that all public relations is handled externally.
- The organization needs specialist services.
- To supply a media-relations service.
- To plan and execute a public relations programme.
- Convenience. If an organization has several offices a consultancy can provide centrally based services for organizing functions such as press launches, conferences and receptions.
- To handle 'one-off' assignments.
- To provide specialist services such as house journal production, corporate or financial public relations and parliamentary PR sponsorship.

In the United Kingdom there are a considerable number of consult-ancies, ranging from the very large, internationally based, to the more modest, medium sized or very small. There are also individual PR practitioners, some of whom offer specialized consultancy services on a business-to-business basis, while others provide more general coverage and a 'full service' for their clients, directly to the public.

About 120 consultancies in this country, who between them probably control about 70 per cent of the total UK consultancy business, are members of the Public Relations Consultants Association (PRCA) that was established to raise and maintain professional and ethical standards in consultancy practice in the UK. For a consultancy to become eligible for membership of the PRCA it has to pass the Consultancy Management Standard (CMS) Assessment. This is a comprehensive assessment covering all areas of reputable business operation reflecting the objectives in the PRCA's mission statement:

- To raise and maintain ethical and professional standards in consultancy practice.
- To provide facilities for government, public bodies associations representing industry, trade and others to confer with public relations consultants as a body.
- To promote confidence in consultancy work and public relations as a whole and act as spokesman for consultancy practice.
- To educate potential clients, establishing the reputation of professionalism of members who conform to our Professional Charter.
- To promote that there is a professional practices committee to oversee standards and arbitrate on complaints.
- To offer practical industry-wide training and development services.
- To monitor and react to perceptions amongst key opinion-leaders.
- To provide a forum on key PR industry issues.
- To demonstrate the effectiveness of good PR in consultancy work.
- To increase opportunities for members to develop new business.
- To improve co-operation with fellow professional bodies in the UK and worldwide.
- To help members improve their efficiency, understanding, skills, professionalism and ethics.

To become eligible for membership a 75 per cent pass rate in the assessment has to be achieved.

TYPES OF CONSULTANCY

The following are the main types, or categories, of consultancy in the UK:

The public relations department of an advertising agency

The department may be limited in scope and service due to being constrained by the agency. Its value depends on how much and how well the agency understands public relations and how much independence they allow the department. Sometimes its work can be no more than publicity support for advertising but, if properly used, it can have considerable influence on market thinking within the agency.

The public relations subsidiary of an agency

This is an independent consultancy in its own right. It has its own clients (who may or may not be agency clients) and is responsible for its own profitability. It has linked directors, usually one or two main board members, and may well operate under a different name to that of the agency.

The independent public relations consultancy

Normally, this type of consultancy has no 'parental ties', but may have links with, or be part of, a larger group. It may also have a working arrangement with an advertising agency, as its clients may need specialist services in addition to those of public relations.

Public relations consultants/counsellors

These are usually individuals who offer no more than a counselling or consultancy service. They may be called in to give advice on a specific area of operation, or as an external independent opinion on internal public relations activities. Certain larger agencies and consultancies may also offer this service.

ADVANTAGES OF USING A CONSULTANCY

Consultancies can offer independent advice through a range of services. Thus they can criticize as well as please the client. As 'outsiders' they are much more objective and can often become the 'guardians' of the client organization's reputation. In addition they can cover many topics with advice, both internally and externally, through trained, qualified and experienced staff. They offer a professional service, and they can be checked on to confirm this – or otherwise!

DISADVANTAGES OF USING A CONSULTANCY

Public relations concerns the internal and external communication of an organization. A consultancy usually works to one person in the organization – the 'liaison officer'. This can sometimes lead to a sense of remoteness and a lack of any effective communication between the client and the consultancy.

The client will only get what he or she pays for – a number of hours' work. But because public relations is often continuous and is integral to any organization, it may not always work 'office hours'. A consultancy may therefore only be able to offer a partial service, depending on the terms of its contract.

A consultancy may not, initially at any rate, be familiar with the 'culture' of the client organization. Sometimes this culture plays a very important part in the work ethic of the organization and ignorance of it can adversely affect the consultancy's relationships with the client.

MIXING AND MATCHING

There are occasions when it may be more appropriate – and cost effective – to use a combination of both the existing in-house resources and a consultancy for specific tasks. This is often the case in large organizations, where the special skills and experience of the consultancy can complement those of the in-house team.

When there is only a small in-house team the use of a consultancy for a specific project or programme is quite common and can be more cost effective than taking on extra staff.

For further detailed information about public relations consultancies and the role of the PRCA you can telephone them on 0207 233 6026, or look them up on their Web site at: www.prca.org.uk.

3

Ethics and the law

Every society has to live by certain rules, standards and codes of behaviour. All of us, whether in our work or in our private life, are expected to have certain standards of behaviour and we expect those with whom we have dealings to have them too. In other words we are expected, and we expect others, to behave in an 'ethical' way.

This chapter looks at the ethical considerations of public relations work and those aspects of the law that can, and often do, affect us. It is meant only as a guide and not a comprehensive legal *aide-mémoire*.

ETHICS

Ethics are defined as being those 'moral principles or set of moral values held by an individual or group'. Ethical conduct is defined in the *Oxford English Dictionary* as being those standards that 'in accordance with principles of conduct are considered correct, especially those of a given profession or group'.

CODES OF CONDUCT

Every professional body, organization, profession or trade body in the UK has its ethical standards, or codes of conduct, by which it expects its members to abide. The Institute of Public Relations (IPR) is no exception.

One of the main objectives of the Institute, as set out in its constitution, is 'to establish and prescribe standards of professional and ethical conduct and ensure the observance of such standards'. The complete IPR Code of Conduct, brought up to date in 2000 and regularly reviewed, is contained in Appendix 1. The code clearly sets out what is, and is not, expected of members in all their dealings.

THE LAW

Everyone who works in public relations needs to have a basic knowledge of those parts of the law that can, and often do, affect his or her areas of work. Some detail on these aspects is given in Appendix 2.

Society has become much more litigious in recent years and defamation cases are now becoming commonplace, with enormous sums of money being awarded in settlement. Today, more than ever, there are so many different ways in which the unwary can get caught up in a legal wrangle or break the law unwittingly. Hence the need for information on those parts of the law which relate to our work.

In this context it is worth remembering that when the term 'the law of the land' is used in documents such as agreements, contracts and codes of conduct, it is referring to the law in England, Wales and Northern Ireland, but *not* Scotland, where the law is somewhat different.

Defamation

This concerns the publication of a statement that purports to bring into disrepute the reputation of a person, organization or product. In English law there are two types of defamation: Slander, the transitory spoken word, and Libel, the written word (which includes radio and television). It is part of civil law and can result in an action for damages.

This is the area where the PR practitioner is most likely to be at risk of causing offence, however innocently. The problem usually arises from material issued to the media, or merely made public, resulting in a civil action being brought against the practitioner, his or her employer, or client. This can not only be damaging to the reputation of the practitioner, employer or client, but can also be very expensive and even, on occasions, ruinous.

Contracts

This is another area where, again, lack of even basic knowledge can lead to litigation, industrial tribunals and civil court cases, with large sums of money changing hands. Contracts affect almost all aspects of public relations work, from simple letters or telephone calls to full written, formal contracts for work or employment.

The terms of each contract will vary, but it is important to ensure that the terms are not only implicit – some are in law – but are also clearly set out so that they can be agreed by both parties.

A model form of client agreement is shown in Appendix 3.

Passing off

This is an aspect of the law which can affect practitioners and their clients, again sometimes with damaging results. It is the misuse of a trade name or of the trade name of goods. It also covers the imitation, or the 'get-up', of the items concerned. The 'get-up' includes the type, size and shape of a container, the labelling and packaging of the goods concerned. Many well-established firms such as the Kellogg Corporation and CPC International Inc. (the makers of Marmite and Bovril) have, over many years, guarded the distinctive 'get-up' of their products very successfully against imitations.

Two examples of recent cases which ended in the High Court include the action brought in 1995 by dress designer Liza Bruce against Marks & Spencer, which produced copies of her swimwear and t-shirts, using slightly different material and colour – but at a much lower price.

The second was the action where the Coca-Cola Corporation were also successful in forcing the supermarket chain, Sainsbury's, to change the appearance – the 'get-up' – of their own-brand cola. It was alleged that confusion was being caused to customers wishing to purchase Coca-Cola because of the similarity.

Details of the law affecting lotteries and competitions are contained in Appendix 2.

COPYRIGHT LAW

Copyright subsists in any original work, but *not* in an idea. In the United Kingdom it is subject to the Copyright, Design and Patents Act 1988 (the Act), which came into force in August 1989. There is a great deal of detail involved and it is worth getting hold of a copy of the synopsis. Copyright is automatic, it does not have to be applied for, but should be declared wherever and whenever possible. Generally, copyright covers the following areas of work:

- original literary, dramatic, musical or artistic work;
- sound recordings, films, broadcasts or cable programmes;
- typographical arrangements of published editions, including:
  - written or printed work;
  - CDs and disc records;
  - photographs;
  - pictures;
  - drawings and illustrations;
  - artwork of all descriptions;
  - broadcast material;
  - video and audio tapes;
  - original literary, dramatic musical or artistic works.

Qualification

The Act is limited in its effects to the UK (and colonies to which it may be extended by Order in Council). It is primarily aimed at protecting the works of British citizens.

Duration

Copyright in literary, artistic, musical or dramatic work expires 70 years after the end of the calendar year in which the author died. This follows the implementation of an EC Directive, 93/98, effective from 1 January 1996, which extended the duration from 50 years. This directive has had the effect of bringing back into copyright many works which, under the Act, were no longer protected. If you are in any doubt you should consult a lawyer with the appropriate experience.

Ownership

The general rule is that a work will be initially owned by its author, the author being the creator of the work or, in the case of a film or sound recording, the person who makes the arrangements necessary for it to be made. One essential exception to this rule is that copyright in the work of an employee produced in the course of his or her employment will belong to his or her employer, except by any agreement to the contrary.

Assignment of copyright

Ownership of copyright is to prevent exploitation of the work. However, the rights to the work can be sold with the owner retaining no interest in it, apart from perhaps royalties. This is called an Assignment of Rights (see Appendix 3).

Alternatively, the owner may grant a licence to another to exploit the work, whilst retaining ownership.

Any agreements dealing with copyright must be quite clear as to whether an assignment of rights or a licence is being granted. Any assignment must be in writing. It can be in the form of a letter and must be signed by, or on behalf of, the assignor. Licences can either be in writing or granted orally. However, an exclusive licence must be in writing.

Moral rights

A new departure from the previous work is the issue of 'moral rights'. This gives the author or director of the work the right to be identified as such in a number of different situations, mainly when the work is being published, performed or otherwise commercially exploited.

Permission to copy

Under the Act, permission must always be obtained for the reproduction and/or use of any copyright written work which comprises any of the following:

- an extract of more than 400 words in length;
- a series of extracts that total more than 800 words;
- a series of extracts where a single extract is more than 300 words;
- an extract, or series of extracts, that comprise more than one-quarter of the whole work.

Provided that permission is sought, it may be that in certain circumstances the publishers and authors will not press for a fee or refuse to give permission. Nonetheless, permission should always be sought, if only as a matter of courtesy. It may also save legal and publishing problems later.

Fair dealing

This is the exception to permission to copy and applies where the material used is not a substantial part of the original work, or its use is educational, or if it is not to be used commercially or for profit. Under these circumstances only due acknowledgement is required, as being both desirable and courteous.

Credits

Giving credit in some sort of form of acknowledgement is a polite and wise thing to do. This is usually done in a list at the beginning, in the preface, or sometimes at the end of the publication. It applies equally to books and publications and to video and film material.

If any part of your work looks as though it might involve you in any sort of legal problems, or if you are in any doubt – check with a lawyer.

4

Working with suppliers

Suppliers of goods and services come in all shapes and sizes, and include photographers, designers and graphic artists, exhibition contractors, video production firms, venue and conference organizers, to mention just a few. They are vital to our work, but to get the best out of them one or two ground rules need to be observed. A guide to dealing with them is given in this chapter.

THE BRIEF

When using suppliers or contractors of any sort it is important that you know and understand exactly what you expect from them and that they understand what they are expected to produce for you. Briefs should always be:

- written;
- comprehensive;
- clear and concise.

A brief should tell the contractor/supplier exactly what you want them to supply – or do. It will be the main point of reference between you and your supplier/contractor. The detail of the brief will also usually form the principal part of any contract (see below).

Verbal briefs can be used, but if you do this it is best to subsequently confirm the brief in writing. This way there will be less chance of misunderstanding and subsequent errors and omissions. Often, a verbal briefing given at the same time as a written one will save time and unnecessary questions.

THE CONTRACT OR AGREEMENT

When drawing up any contract, or agreement:

● Keep it as simple as possible.
● Make sure it says what *you* want it to say.
● Avoid legal or any other sort of jargon wherever possible.

A contract or agreement should be specific in its wording – not vague, nor open to possible misunderstanding, nor to being misconstrued, neither should it be open ended (see Appendix 3). Remember to check for any financial regulations you may have in your organization (eg work costing over a certain amount automatically going out to tender).

It is good practice to get any contract or agreement checked out by your legal department.

TIMETABLING

It may be that there are deadlines that have to be worked to by your supplier, such as production of published material in time for a launch. If so, you should make quite sure that he or she understands what these are and that the timetabling for publication is included in any agreement. Penalty clauses can be incorporated if necessary.

Always allow for emergencies. If, for example, you are preparing publication of a book for launching on a certain date, try to build some 'leeway', or extra time, into your overall publication timetable. This allows for any emergencies, such as the printers telling you that their machines have 'gone down' at the critical moment, or for any distribution problems.

COSTINGS

Costings should be as accurate and as detailed as you can get them. If you are working within an overall budget figure then you will have to 'cut your coat to suit the cloth'. If you can, have a 'contingency' fund to allow for any sudden last-minute changes of plan or cost increases beyond your control.

VAT

Don't forget VAT which, if not allowed for, can have a devastating effect on your budget. If you can claim it back, all well and good, but check for any exemptions that may apply. It may be worth getting hold of a copy of *Croner's Guide to VAT Regulations* if you are in doubt. It could save you a lot of money in the long run.

PROGRESS CHASING

Pressure may have to be kept on the contractor/supplier to ensure that the agreed timetable is adhered to. Regular meetings to check on progress are important because, if there are problems, the timetable may have to be revised. Overruns may involve him or her in penalty clauses.

5

Working with publishers

If you have written a book and you are able to fund both production and printing costs yourself, you can just use a printer to produce it for you. This may sound simple, but you must always remember that if you want to achieve substantial sales, printers will not handle any of the distribution or promotion costs. Therefore, it may be best to approach a publisher. There are several ways of doing this. Some publishers may be willing to fund your project if they think it to be commercially viable and it fits with their editorial policy. If you do decide to use a publisher, first make sure you select one that works in your field. Publishers are very specific and will only handle particular types of books.

On the other hand, it may be to your advantage to approach a book packager. This is a publisher who not only produces books, but also who sometimes distributes and promotes books funded by someone else.

You can always check this out in the current edition of the *Writers' & Artists' Yearbook*. This gives details of the types of book published by each publisher, or packager, together with the names of contacts.

THE BRIEF

If you are going to use a publisher, you normally have to submit a sample chapter and a synopsis to either the commissioning editor, or the acquisitions editor. Unsolicited manuscripts are only rarely accepted for publication. However, if the commissioning editor does accept the proposal, you will then be given a detailed brief to follow to complete and submit your final manuscript. This can be done verbally at a meeting, but should always be confirmed in writing as soon as possible thereafter, to prevent any subsequent misunderstanding. The brief will be very specific. It will include, for example, the number, type, extent and the tone, etc, of any illustrations.

THE CONTRACT

The contract can be either as simple as a formal letter or it can be a very precise and detailed legal document. It should set out the agreed terms: your royalty payments, the details of the manuscript, deadline for submission, etc. Make sure that any distribution and promotion details are clearly and unequivocally stated. Any assignment of copyright, or licence to rights, should also be included.

Get the contract, or the letter, checked first by a legal person, preferably one who is familiar with the law of copyright.

THE MANUSCRIPT

Normally the submitted manuscript should be typed on single sides of A4, in double spacing. These days the text is often submitted on computer 'floppy' disc or CD ROM together with a printed or 'hard' copy. However, there may be other special requirements to be met, which may be quite detailed. The publisher will usually tell you what they are in written guidelines. Particularly, you should not include any 'design' elements in your typed text. For instance, do not use centred text, indents, different typefaces, etc, as this will slow up the production process.

Copy editing

After your manuscript has been accepted for publication, it will be given to a copy editor who will read and check it in detail, edit it for consistency and adherence to the publisher's house style, perhaps suggesting changes of wording to improve readability. You may well be involved in helping to resolve queries at this stage.

Proofs and illustrations

You will be sent a first proof of the text of your publication from the publisher. Proofs should always be read very carefully, to check for errors and omissions. The publisher will also normally use a professional proof-reader. This is also the time to make any essential, last minute, alterations to the text, but not stylistic improvements. You may also, at this stage, need to prepare the index.

Having done this, you will then get a final proof, showing the page layout, position of any illustrations, the index and details such as the cover design.

Illustrations

You should consider any illustrations you want when preparing the text, as well as where you want them placed. They can either be spread throughout the text or grouped together in the middle of the publication. All pictures should be clearly captioned. When reading the proofs, ensure that any illustrations you select are not printed back to front, particularly photographs! Always check with the publishers first regarding illustrations – they may have special requirements.

If you are able to supply the necessary photographs yourself then these may be used, but always make sure that they are of suitable quality for reproduction. Otherwise, the publisher will have to employ a picture researcher to find appropriate photographs either from picture agencies or from other commercial sources.

Colour photographs are best reproduced from colour transparencies. Colour prints do not usually reproduce well in black and white – they tend to look slightly blurred, as though shot in soft focus.

If in any doubt, talk to a professional photographer first, or ask advice from the publisher's production specialists.

Artwork

If you are using artwork (ie graphics, charts, drawings – line drawings, cartoons or any original illustrations) you may be able to supply 'camera ready' artwork, or computer generated artwork that is suitable for reproduction. Usually, however, the publisher will have artwork prepared by professional artists, using your drawings as roughs.

You will be sent proofs of the redrawn artwork to check. When checking final page proofs, always check that the details, colours and positioning of any artwork are as you wanted them.

PROMOTION AND DISTRIBUTION

The responsibilities of the publisher normally include both the promotion and the distribution of the publication in question. Any specific responsibilities for these areas should be quite clearly stated in any agreement or contract.

Depending on the terms of the agreement, a packager will normally take either a percentage of the unit sale price or a fixed sum per sale. A publisher, on the other hand, will pay you a royalty. This is usually a percentage of the unit sale price and payable at six-monthly intervals.

6

Working with printers

BACKGROUND

It may be preferable to use a printer direct, instead of a publisher. Apart from being more economical, it can also sometimes be more appropriate, as you have direct contact and can therefore have more control over the outcome. However, it also means more 'hands on' work for you!

There are a wide range of different types of printing companies available, offering a vast array of services: digital colour proofing, short-run on-demand digital printing (this allows for personalization of individual sheets), conventional lithographic and gravure printing as well as a wide range of finishing.

Printing is quite a complicated process. If you have no previous experience in this field, and before deciding which printer to use, a visit to a number of printing works can give you an insight into their capabilities. Ask to see work they have carried out for other clients, and check with those customers, too. Get estimates from several printers based on a precise and carefully specified brief, so as to compare like with like.

Most printers have some in-house design capabilities within their organization, although they may not normally provide design services as such. However, a good printer can give advice on matters such as page layout, from the technical, printing point of view, but design concepts, the overall style, typeface to be used, layout and make-up will be left to you. You should also get paper samples (see below).

There is an increasing amount of out-sourced work that comes together at the printer. Recently, the use of digital artwork has become the norm. It is now possible to encapsulate all your digital files into Adobe's portable document file (PDF). This keeps all your graphics, pictures and fonts together. PDFs are transferable across different computer platforms as compact files.

THE BRIEF AND THE CONTRACT

As with publishers, the brief and the subsequent contract should clearly state your requirements: what it is you want the printer to do. Brief, either in writing (the client brief), or verbally, and discuss your requirements. Follow this with a letter of confirmation, which should include any technical specifications you have agreed. This will prevent subsequent misunderstandings and can also serve as the contract, or the basis of one.

ILLUSTRATIONS

The same rules apply here as they do with publishers. Check with them first, as you need to know if they have any specific requirements. Some printers may be able to produce graphics, such as pie charts, graphs, etc, themselves, based on your statistics. Alternatively, they may prefer you to produce the finished artwork. Often, you can get your photographer and graphics artist to liaise with the printer directly over technical details. A discussion with your printer or a graphic designer can be helpful, and is often very productive.

PAPER SPECIFICATION

This is a very complex subject, as there is a wide variety of paper on the market, including recycled, laid or woven papers, different types of card and 'board', all with different colours, thicknesses and finishes. Talk to your printer at an early stage. He or she can help you in your choice.

7

Working with photographers

Good, innovative, well-presented photography can make all the difference to a job. It will complement and enhance the finished product, whether it is a publication, brochure, display, backdrop or an exhibition. It is therefore worth spending the time, and the money, in making sure you get it right.

CHOOSING A PHOTOGRAPHER

There are many different types and categories of photographers working today. They range from the generalist, freelance or press photographer, to the specialist who only works in one specific field.

When choosing a photographer, it is 'horses for courses'. Each one is, hopefully, expert in his or her own field. Usually freelance, they are often listed in trade directories. Depending on what, or who, you want to have photographed, select the most appropriate. You may already have a list of those with whom you have worked before;

if so, you will know who you want and with whom you can work best.

If you have not commissioned a photographer before, then your own personal networking contacts may be able to help you, or you can look in directories. There are a number of very useful publications available that can point you in the right direction such as *The Artists' & Writers' Yearbook*, an excellent reference guide, and *The Directory of Picture Libraries and Agencies*. The latter is published by the British Association of Picture Libraries and Agencies (BAPLA) in London and is also available on their Web site at www.bapla.org (see also below, under Photographic libraries).

Specialist journals and trade magazines, such as the current edition of *The Artists' & Writers' Yearbook* already mentioned, *PR Week*, *Adline*, *Campaign*, etc, may also be able to provide useful names and contacts. The Royal Photographic Society may also be able to offer advice. You can contact them either by phone on 01225 462841, by e-mail at rps@rps.org, or on their Web site at www.rps.org.

PHOTOGRAPHIC LIBRARIES

Instead of going to the expense of hiring a photographer yourself, you can, if you prefer, use a photo library. These libraries will normally provide catalogues free on request, with a wide variety of 'stock' shots. These are special collections of generic, topical pictures, in black and white or colour, covering categories such as children, young people, the elderly, houses, business, architecture, transport etc. Photo libraries can supply transparencies equal to, and often superior to, shots from even the best assignment photographers. The cost of using shots from photo libraries is often a fraction of what it would be to set up a shoot, hire models, pay location fees, stylists, prop charges etc. Their photos are all taken by often quite famous professional photographers.

In addition, most national, regional and even local newspapers have their own picture libraries. If you find what you want from the catalogue or library, just ring up and ask for the picture. If not, then pick out those libraries which you feel are likely to have what you need and phone them.

If you are quite specific as to the picture you want, most libraries should be able to tell you immediately if they have it. Failing that, you can contact the British Association of Picture Libraries and Agencies who should be able to help. Having got the picture you are looking for you can, for a small fee, view it and then show it to your client.

Fees and agreements

Fees for using the photographs are usually negotiable. Be frank about your budget. Get a quotation beforehand. This will enable you to plan that part of the work.

When you get the photograph, read the rental agreement document carefully. There may be a penalty for keeping it beyond the agreed date. Take good care of it while you have it or you may be charged for damage or loss. Remember, you are responsible for looking after it, so do not lend it out to a third party.

You may only use a photograph or illustration as agreed. For example, to make a second copy of an illustration as part of an advertising flyer may incur additional costs.

COLOUR OR BLACK AND WHITE?

Again, it depends on what you want and how it will be used in the finished product. You should specify in the brief whether all the pictures are to be black and white or colour – or a mixture of both. Also specify the size and the finish. Do you want glossy, matt, sepia, 5×4, 10×8, portrait or landscape? (A 'portrait' picture is upright; 'landscape' is lengthways on.)

LOCATION AND STUDIO WORK

With photographers you either work in a studio setting or out on location. Both require forethought and planning. Remember, you normally pay a photographer by the hour or by the day, plus expenses, so you must make the best use of time – and money. You may also need to hire models and/or props for the work involved. This may involve the use of an agency, or the photographer may have his or her own.

You need to coordinate the details of the shoot with the photographer, such as timings, the hire or loan of props, hiring of any models, transport arrangements, etc.

You might want to use a studio setting for the job, either the photographer's own studio or, if it is not suitable for your task, a hired one.

Location work can be inside or outside. A visit to the proposed location prior to the shoot, with the photographer if possible, is a good idea. It can save trouble later. And, of course, make sure you book the chosen venue for the day and time you want, and can use it without interruptions.

Internal locations

These are usually easier to arrange. However, remember that lighting and other technical apparatus all have to be set up, and props and furniture moved about. Also, you do not want distractions while shooting is in progress, like casual spectators, or, if the shoot is in house, colleagues or anyone else popping their heads round the door. If you are using professional models, remember that they probably have to be collected and returned and that dressing-room facilities, or the equivalent, may be needed.

External locations

These need advance planning in more detail. Again, a reconnaissance before the day to pick suitable locations may be essential, especially if you are using several different ones. Also, you may need special clearance, permission or a fee may be payable to use certain locations, such as a garden, an interior, the front of a building, or a building site. Fees for such use are increasingly charged as a source of income, even on sites that may be considered open to the public. This can have a serious impact on the budget.

Weather watching

On the day, a 'weather watch' may be needed if there is any question about the weather holding. Delays mean money. In the event of wet weather there should be somewhere for everyone to shelter.

Other requirements

Methods and modes of transport, 'transit' timings (how long it takes to get between A and B), catering, any special requirements, etc, all need to be considered. Changing facilities may also be required, although this would be somewhat unusual – unless you are doing a fashion or a costume shoot.

CONTACT SHEETS, TRANSPARENCIES OR DIGITAL?

When the shoot is complete you want to see the finished product – the photographs themselves. You are entitled to see all the pictures taken, not just the photographer's own short list of 'possibles'. You should agree beforehand how they are to be presented to you. They will come normally in the form of a contact sheet, or sheets, each sheet being the equivalent of a roll of film. No commercial photographers normally use 35mm film with the standard 24 or 36 exposures. They use either 120mm (roll) film, or 5×4 plates. 120mm film means 10 or 12 exposures to the roll. Occasionally it may be 20, or even 24 exposures, but this is rare. To look at contact sheets successfully, and meaningfully, you need to have a magnifying lens, which you use much as a jeweller uses a jeweller's glass, in order to see all the detail in the photo.

If you ask for colour transparencies you will need to be able to look at them through a light box. This enables you to see many, if not all, of the transparencies at the same time. Otherwise you have to hold them up to the light – not always the best way! If you have your own light box, so much the better, as you can view the transparencies privately. Otherwise ask to use the photographer's.

If you are having prints made, then make your selection, usually in conjunction with the photographer. Give him or her details of the sizes required, what kind of finish you want, any 'cropping' required for the picture to fit the frame, etc.

It is also possible for images to be photographed and supplied digitally. This uses equipment similar to the compact digital camera, but working to a much higher specification. The film would then be supplied on a computer disc, such as a CD ROM, and would need to be viewed on a computer with the appropriate software.

If you are going to use transparencies, the photographer will supply them. They are unique and irreplaceable. If they get scratched they will be unusable.

SPECIAL EFFECTS

There are many different types of finish for photographs today, all of which can be used to enhance illustrative work depending on the situation. Photographs do not have to be only in a black-and-white, or colour, format. Clever use of special effects can enhance an otherwise dull publication.

Often, old photographs or those of a historical nature look better in a sepia finish. There are many effects that can be used by the photographer, such as soft focus, high key, etc, or by the printer's platemaker. This process is called 'posterization'. If what is known as half-tone is to be used, bear in mind that it is not as the name suggests, but rather that it prints the full range of tones. There is also the effect known as 'knockback'. This is the technique of fading the photograph – either a black and white or a colour image – into the background so that it is almost only an impression. Another image, usually writing, can then be superimposed on top.

When you hear photographers talking about 'bleeding' they are merely referring to the technique where the photograph surmounts one or more edges of the page.

If you feel special effects are needed then you should discuss them with the photographer or printer, or get a designer to advise you.

ASSIGNMENT OF COPYRIGHT

Remember that under the terms of the Copyright, Design and Patents Act 1988 the owner of the copyright of any work is the author or creator of it, in this case the photographer. The only exception to this is where that work is created in the course of employment, when the copyright belongs to the employer. However, when a photograph is commissioned the photographer can be asked to agree an assignment of copyright, as one of the terms of that commission. Therefore, if you wish to own the copyright, you must have an assignment of copyright put in the contract (see Appendix 3).

Fair dealing

This covers the reuse of material for reporting and maintains that if a picture is essentially a straight copy of all or part of the original work, copyright in the work remains and the photographer's rights under the Act and/or licence to rights must be observed.

Moral rights

Photographers have a right to prevent any derogatory treatment of their pictures, such as selective cropping or slanted captions, except when used in a newspaper, magazine or encyclopaedia. Derogatory use also covers inappropriate use, eg inferior reproduction from contact sheets.

REPRODUCTION STUDIOS

These studios operate in most major towns and cities, and can be very useful to you. The imaging business continues to develop, and today most photographic reproduction studios can provide a comprehensive service in an ever-changing market place. Many now offer a range of image manipulation services and high resolution output, as well as such services as photographic direct print from print systems, up to A4 size, within one working day.

They specialize in all forms of photographic work, developing, printing, transparencies, slides, overhead projector transparencies, artwork from computer-generated originals, enlargement to almost any size, heat sealing, mounting and many other techniques. If you do not already know of one, find out where they are, visit them to find out their range of services, and get a price list.

8

Working with designers

BACKGROUND

Designers and design consultancies often specialize in particular areas of design work and, like all creative people, they each have particular expertise and experience in their own field. Although many companies tend to use the design capabilities of the larger design consultancies, there are a growing number of small design consultancies that are very competitive. Because they are comparatively new in the industry they often have fresh ideas and an innovative approach to design work.

When commissioning a design team, find out first if their specialisms match your needs. Check on other work they have done. Is their style what you are looking for, or is it too conservative or too *avant-garde*? The choice you make will be all important to the finished product, whether it is a strap for a publication, a house style or a complete exhibition stand.

If you are unsure and don't really know where to start, the Design Council and the Society of Chartered Designers both have design registers that provide information on consultancies in each area of design practice. They can help you in choosing the right one. However, at the end of the day, your final choice will depend on the design consultancies' presentations when they pitch for the business.

DESKTOP PUBLISHING

Much design work today is now computer based and generated, and many designers use desktop publishing (DTP) systems to assist them in their work. This, of course, can be very effective and time saving, always providing that the result is exactly what *you* want, and not something that was DTP-produced because it was an easy way of designing.

THE BRIEF

The brief should always reflect your aims and objectives and lay down clear operating guidelines. Designers are 'problem solvers' and therefore it is better to give them the problem and let them give you their answer. That is what they are getting paid for! However, there is no harm in you outlining your concepts and thoughts to the design team, as part of the brief.

You may find out just how good the consultancy is from the way they take your brief, ie how and what they ask in the way of questions. When you discuss the brief with the designer(s) you must resolve the stages of the job and also the method of payment, ie by stages, upfront or in arrears. *Make sure this is included in the contract document.* If the designer, like you, is a member of a professional body (such as the Chartered Institute of Designers) then he or she will be bound by their code of conduct. So, of course, will you!

The brief should include the following information:

- clear aims and objectives;
- background information on your organization;
- any existing work or house style that may help the design team in their work;
- any constraints in operation, eg an existing in-house design manual for detailing corporate colours, logo, typeface etc;
- target audiences;

- useful contacts for research purposes;
- budget;
- timetable.

THE WORK

Roughs

Initially the designer will come back to you with 'roughs' of the design solution (see Figure 8.1). These are the designer's first ideas, based on the brief and your previous discussions with the design team. Usually in the form of pencil or pen and ink sketches, 'roughs' can actually be quite sophisticated, and may include such things as models, mock-ups and 'dummy' page layouts.

They are intended to give you some idea of the way the design team sees the concept, and for you to discuss these first thoughts with them. At this stage, nothing is cast in tablets of stone.

If you like what you see, well and good. They can proceed to the next stage. However, if you do *not* like what you see, then now is the time to say so. Do not be overawed by designers or their jargon into accepting something that does not meet your requirements. If need be, it will have to be 'back to the drawing-board' for them.

Finished artwork/final proofs

This is the next stage, following approval of the roughs. Drawings, or designs, will have been produced in a 'finished' or final proof state, ie in full colour, layout etc, ready to be printed, assembled, or put on display.

Major changes to text or design at this stage may incur extra charges, since additional work has to be carried out. A whole page layout, design solution or display layout may have to be scrapped and started again.

In the case of exhibition designs, you should always see a final artist's impression of the design for the stand prior to its actually being constructed. You should then see it assembled, prior to its being dismantled for transporting to the venue (see Figure 8.2).

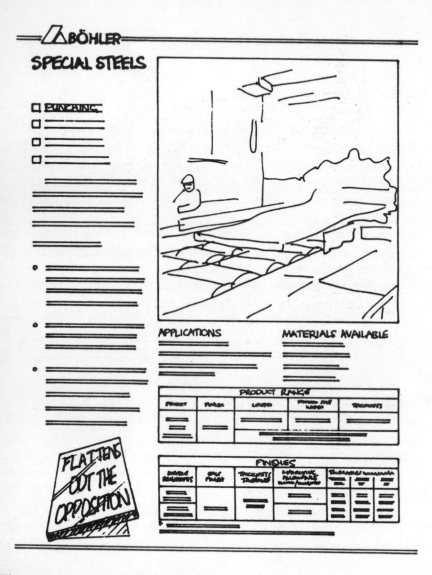

Figure 8.1 *A rough design sketch*

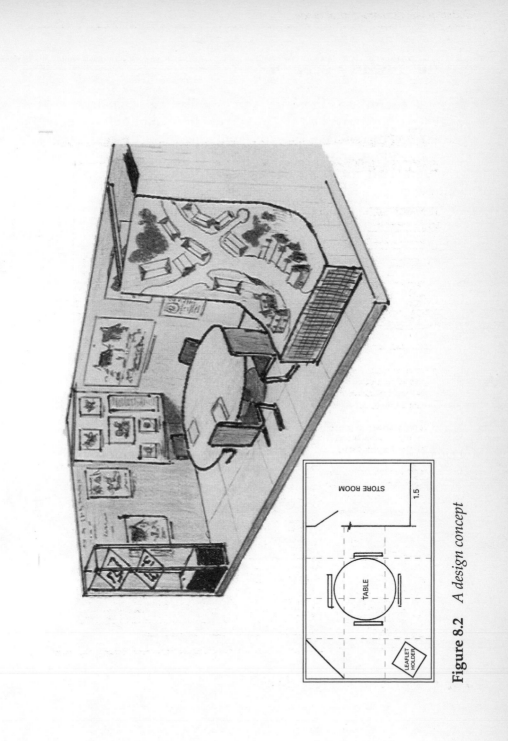

Figure 8.2 *A design concept*

Camera-ready artwork

This is the term used in printing and publishing when artwork is ready to be photographed and put on to film as part of the printing process. You do not have to be too familiar with the process, as your designer will be, and if some form of artwork for a publication is being produced, then let the design consultancy liaise directly with your printer.

CONCLUSION

These, then, are some of the points that need to be borne in mind when using designers, whether from large consultancies, design houses or individuals. Remembering them will help you to understand the various stages and the processes involved.

9

Making videos

INTRODUCTION

The use of videos is now an accepted part of public relations work. As the technology improves and becomes increasingly economical, it is becoming much more commonly used as a promotional, educational and information tool. There will be times, therefore, when the production of a video becomes the responsibility of the public relations department, or the task of the consultancy.

Various steps have to be taken, in order that the outcome, ie the finished product, is both cost effective and fulfils the requirements that have been set out, either by the client or by the in-house management policies.

THE FILM MAKERS

Unless you work for an organization big enough to have its own in-house video production team and camera crew, the usual procedure is to use one of the many video production companies, or an independent film maker.

Use the phone book to find a local company or person or, if the video calls for very specialized treatment, then you may need a specialist production house. They often advertise in *PR Week*, or in other related trade magazines. When you have some names, check them out if possible with previous clients, and/or look at some of their previous work. These will be the best – and the most reliable – references you can get.

COSTS

A word here about costings. These may vary enormously, depending on the type, length and quality of video you require. If it needs lots of location work then expect the costs to reflect this. The use of professional actors also puts the price up smartly.

However, with skilful use of any available 'still' material, plus a bit of location work and a reasonable 'voice over', the cost can be kept to a reasonable level. What, then, can be described as 'reasonable'?

A rule of thumb when costing out a video production in normal circumstances (ie not filming abroad in exotic locations, or extensively from the air, or anything similar) is that it is calculated at about £1,000 per minute of screening time. Thus, a 20-minute video, the average running time for most PR videos, will cost in the order of £20,000 plus VAT. This cost should include script writing, filming, location work, post-production studio work, voice-overs, end titles and any music.

THE CONCEPT

Equivalent to the theme in a feature article, the concept gives the film maker the overall 'bottom-line' objectives: what is to be achieved, what messages put over, and how it is to be done. This is not in detail (that is the producer's job, together with the script writer and director), but in the overall context. It is worth spending time to make sure that the producer and script writer are quite clear on this.

The producer/director should come back with 'story boards'. These are rough sketches showing how the sequences of the filming will be put together to give the story. They help the producer and the director plan their filming schedules, locations etc.

THE SCRIPT

It may be that writing the entire script is left to the script writer – usually a professional freelance journalist or writer – with the client merely seeing and approving the finished product. On the other hand, the script may call for input from the client, who may have some specialized knowledge and understanding about the subject that the script writer does not have. The script writer will carry out research prior to any writing taking place, with or without the client's input.

A copy of the draft should be sent to the client well in advance, certainly in time for it to be checked. Always ensure that the necessary research *has* been carried out, and check the script carefully for inaccuracies, prior to the start of filming.

FILMING

You can, and should, request a shooting schedule. This is the time-table of filming and will be flexible, particularly if there has to be a 'weather watch' for outside location work. It is also useful for making arrangements, so that anyone who is to be involved can be forewarned and any special requirements, permissions, clearances etc can be made.

If possible a liaison person from the client's company should be with the film crew, if only to act as a link and able to handle anything untoward happening on location. When filming is completed it may be possible to view the 'rushes', ie the various bits of film, before they are edited into the finished product.

POST-PRODUCTION

Editing

Carried out by the production house in an editing 'suite' in their studio, this is where all filmed material is put together, edited down, and any music, end titles and voice over added prior to a final run through.

The client is normally invited to this preview to see the finished work and to give approval. At this stage, minor alterations can still be made if necessary.

Packaging the finished product

Depending on what the video has been made for, it may be necessary to have a special, decorative cover made for the video box, together with a stick-on label on the cassette itself. These may have to be specifically designed, either by the studio (with additional cost implications), or in-house by the client. Alternatively, a simple typed label may be sufficient if the video is only to be used in house for, say, training purposes. Whichever way, it needs a bit of thought.

10

Exhibitions and other events

This chapter covers some of the higher profile work in which public relations practitioners get involved from time to time. All these areas, exhibitions, displays and events, generally involve an enormous amount of planning, attention to detail and above all hard work.

The chapter does not cover working abroad, where planning details can vary enormously according to the host country, location, type of exhibition, promotion or trade fair etc. However, the general principles remain the same. What follows are a number of hints, tips and checklists which should be useful to the reader.

EXHIBITIONS AND TRADE FAIRS

There is always a pubic relations benefit to be gained from exhibitions, whether they are large or small, an international trade fair, private view, public exhibition, or even a local carnival or fête.

Remember the difference between a trade show and an exhibition – exhibitions are open to the public, trade shows are normally restricted to the trade. There are exceptions to this rule, however, with major events such as the Motor Show and the Boat Show which, although primarily aimed at business, are also open to the public.

Characteristics

Large exhibitions and trade fairs have the same general character-istics. They take place at well-known venues, eg Olympia, Earls Court or the NEC. They have large, often very sophisticated, stands and displays. They usually last between three and five days (some-times even longer), take months of preparation and, while they can be exciting and fun (especially if in some exotic location abroad!), are usually exhausting work for all concerned.

Above all else, there is the opportunity at exhibitions and trade fairs to meet your 'publics' and get to know them, so that when you contact them afterwards you are not just a voice at the other end of a telephone, but a person with whom they have had personal contact.

The different types of work

From the public relations practitioner's point of view, there are four aspects of involvement in exhibition work. They are:

1. public relations support at an exhibition stand;
2. setting up and running a stand at an exhibition;
3. organizing an exhibition;
4. public relations exhibitions or displays.

SUPPORT AT THE STAND

The value of any exhibition is enhanced by taking full advantage of any public relations opportunities that can be created. These oppor-tunities must never be neglected or overlooked. If you have been commissioned, either as the PR department in an organization which is exhibiting, or by your client as a consultancy, to give public rela-tions support on the stand, there are some basic rules to remember.

Before the event takes place, you need to have some details, such as:

- The organization exhibiting – is it part of a larger group or conglomerate, or is it an independent exhibitor?
- What are they exhibiting – what is on show?
- Are there any special or unusual features about either the stand or any of the exhibits?
- What handouts or free gifts are available, what special promotional activities etc are scheduled to take place?

Armed with this information, there are a number of activities that have to be carried out when planning, before, during and after the exhibition. These are given in detail in Appendix 5, and include matters such as making contact with the exhibition press office, finding out who is opening the exhibition, getting details about the press day and much more.

SETTING UP AND RUNNING YOUR OWN STAND

When you are responsible for a stand at an exhibition, care must be taken not only in the planning prior to the event, but also in the staffing and in the implementation. After all, you are presenting, or even selling, a professional service on the stand, so why do so in an amateurish way?

Bad planning and slipshod operating of an exhibition stand is bad public relations and the organization being represented on the stand will not be seen to best advantage. An exhibition stand is intended to show off the organization it represents. It should not only look professional, but also be professional in the way it is run. If it is, then it will not only serve to enhance the organization's reputation, but also your own.

Before the event

Good planning is essential for success. If you intend to exhibit, then some key questions need to be answered first, such as:

- What is the purpose of the exhibition?
- Why are we going?
- What sort of image is to be displayed?

- How is it to be achieved?
- What is the budget for it?

Assuming that you get satisfactory answers to these questions and are going ahead, you now book the necessary exhibition space.

Booking space

This is done through exhibition organizers, or contractors. These are specialist firms, expert and experienced in this kind of work. Bookings are taken in advance, normally six months to a year ahead, depending on the event. Trade fairs are often booked a year or more in advance. Early booking should ensure that you get a stand where you can be seen, not one in some dark, out-of-the-way corner. Make sure you are happy with the position of the stand.

On booking, a percentage of the fee is payable up front as a deposit. This may or may not be refundable in the event of cancellation – always check the small print of the contract. The balance of the fee is payable after the event.

What sort of space?

When booking stand space, exhibition organizers will usually offer a choice, either basic stand space or, more expensively, a 'shell stand'. Stand *space* is simply that – you have to produce the stand within the constraints of the space booked. *Shell* stands, on the other hand, come complete with walls, usually of hardboard or similar material, a standard facia board over the front with your organization's name and stand number, some sort of flooring, a ceiling and basic lighting. Make sure the correct details are on the facia.

The rest, as they say, is down to you.

Contractor's manual

Details of the exhibition venue, including specifications of the shell stand construction, height and other restrictions, should all be contained in the contractor's manual. This indispensable document should be sent to you on confirmation of booking space. If it isn't, insist on getting one soonest.

The manual should contain a wealth of detailed information. It tells you what you can and cannot do on the stand, and what additional services are available for hire – such as furnishings, floral decorations, stand cleaning etc. Handy booking forms are enclosed at the back. However, do remember that all these attractive optional extras will cost you! So, if you are working to a tight budget, take your own, or borrow where possible.

The unions

At many exhibition venues the unions involved may have an agreement with the venue management that only qualified persons may put up and take down the stands. Specific rules on this may be laid down and if so, should be in the manual. Check it out. (The author speaks from bitter personal experience having, unintentionally, nearly caused a 24-hour strike at the Brighton Metropole Exhibition Centre by using a screwdriver to fix a light on his stand!)

Unions

Planning the stand

In planning what the stand will look like you can choose either to 'do your own thing' by using existing material, designing your own stand with visual displays, photographs, models, or whatever else you wish. Or you can go the whole hog – if you can afford it – and hire a designer to do it for you.

Exhibition designers

Exhibition designers will design, transport, erect and dismantle the stand to your specific needs. A good exhibition designer can save you money and many hours' work. It may well be more cost efficient to use one, thus allowing you to arrive at the venue fresh and eager to go, knowing that your stand will have been set up for you and that at the end you can walk away from it.

Some designers also provide a range of other services, including special graphics, finishes, logos, photographic panels and much more. They are not cheap, but will work within your budget limits. Basically, you will get what you can afford.

They are professionally qualified and experienced and will be familiar with the venue and any constraints there may be. They also carry the right union cards (see above).

During the exhibition

You should arrive at the venue at least the day before, and carry out the checks relevant to you that are given in Appendix 5.

Press kits and exhibition publications

Press kits

It is not always necessary to produce lavish press kits packed with non-news items. The press will be selective and will only take what they feel they can use. Don't overwhelm them with bits and pieces. Remember, there will be hundreds of stands, all providing their own information. Make sure, however, that the press office is kept topped up with the relevant topical information, handouts, photos etc from your stand. Visiting once or twice a day to check will be helpful. They will get to recognize and know you – good public relations for you!

Exhibition newsletters

During a big exhibition there is normally an exhibition newsletter published. There might only be one edition, but may be two or three depending on the duration of the exhibition. They will want contributions from you. If not, offer some anyway.

News and events

There is usually a daily 'bulletin' issued by the exhibition press office for the exhibitors' convenience. Normally on two sides of A4, it simply gives the events of the current or following day, any special events, visits, or other exhibition news. It is usually circulated to all stands every morning prior to opening up, or the evening before. You may want to get something into it for your own stand. If so, make sure you know when it is required and by whom.

Good housekeeping

Stand cleaning

Exhibition stands can get quite grubby, both from your own staff and from visitors and the rubbish they leave behind. There will be your own litter to be removed, ashtrays to be emptied, plastic cups etc disposed of, and the whole stand generally freshened up on a daily basis.

Do you really want to vacuum up all those crumbs on the floor after that reception, remove those coffee stains and polish up the stand furniture? You can if you want to. If so, you will need to have the necessary cleaning equipment with you – which either has to be stored at the back of the stand or brought in every day. Or you can hire a cleaning service that will do all these chores, which not only saves your time – but your energy too. This service is normally advertised in the contractors' manual and can be booked prior to the event.

Floral decorations

The same also applies to any flowers, foliage etc on the stand. They can be booked in advance and will be delivered complete in their containers to your stand and removed at the end. Or you can provide your own.

Furniture

You can either bring your own, or hire it on site. There are many firms specializing in hiring furniture for stands. They offer a wide range, from chairs and tables to ashtrays, wastepaper baskets and the like.

Afterwards

Don't forget the evaluation or 'wash up'. It will be your benchmark for future similar events. Look at both the good and bad points. Work out what could be done differently – or better – for next time.

ORGANIZING AN EXHIBITION

What happens when the public relations department has to organize, and then run, an exhibition itself? How is it done? Many of the actions required are similar to those given in the section above, but with some major differences. The department (you) becomes responsible for all of the following:

- booking the venue;
- arrangements for all publicity and promotion;
- inviting potential exhibitors to participate;
- providing the contractor's manual;
- arranging the exhibition hall layout and the provision of stand space, services etc;
- manning a press office and providing information services.

Contractors

Much, if not all, of the detailed provision and planning needed to set up an exhibition can be dealt with by employing an exhibition contracting firm. Using such a contractor is very often the best, most cost-effective and professional way to organize an exhibition. They have professionally trained staff, experienced in all aspects of exhibition work. Using one will enable the PR department to co-ordinate all the detailed planning and also make the best use of its own resources, both in terms of time and money.

Used extensively by organizations and trade associations in the UK, they set up and then run professional trade and public exhibitions, both in this country and abroad. They can solve all your problems for you at a stroke. However, they do not come cheap.

The contractor's brief

As there will be very large amounts of money involved, if using such a firm, or firms, ensure that they are always given a clear, comprehensive brief and that the subsequent written agreement contains all the detail.

CONCLUSION

Exhibitions are a very good, and often cost effective, way of promoting an organization's image creatively. They are an excellent way of communicating at first hand with clients, the public and the media, and can show off the exhibitor and whatever products and services are being displayed to the best advantage.

But, because they are also expensive, the reasons for being at a trade fair or exhibiting at some major spectacular events must be carefully considered beforehand, and the expense justified. Some serious decisions have also to be taken as to what messages and images are to be put across, and how to do this within the allocated budget. As with all public relations work, attention to detail is very important in order to ensure success.

The first event is always the worst – with experience it gets a lot easier!

11

Promotions and functions

Promotions and functions cover a wide spectrum of events, from seminars, conferences and annual general meetings to press launches. The management of functions and promotions is an area of public relations work that has grown more sophisticated, and more complicated, during the last decade. As with exhibitions and displays, successful management of promotions and functions generally can be a most effective public relations tool, and one that is becoming more frequently used.

Inevitably, there will be examples of bad planning, slipshod management and execution on the organizational side. Overall, however, the trend in this area of our work is positive, with an increasing number of better managed, often more sophisticated events, and an increased professionalism in the approach to this aspect of public relations work.

VENUES

The choice of venues for functions such as promotions, product launches, conferences and the like is now very varied. In recent years there has been a boom in the building of convention centres all over the country. Many cities and towns have central sites with multi-purpose properties, built for the staging of events. They range from the vast Queen Elizabeth Conference Centre and the Wembley Conference Centre in London, the International Convention Centre in Birmingham, to The Hawth in Crawley and Woburn Abbey in Bedfordshire. Many smaller cities and large towns have converted or newly built properties on central sites for this purpose.

Most decent-sized hotels have purpose-built conference centres and facilities, catering for often quite large events. Even some theatres in London are now promoting their facilities for business entertainment, conferences and product launches. Universities, college campuses, public schools, castles, country houses, racecourses and football stadiums are all gearing up to become venues for conferences and special events throughout the year and are all touting for business.

When choosing a venue, therefore, a number of considerations need to be taken into account. You need to ask yourself the following questions before making a final decision:

- Is the venue appropriate to the event?
- Is it accessible and convenient to get to?
- Is it big enough?
- Does it have enough accommodation?
- Is it the right sort of accommodation?
- What other facilities are there, either at the venue or adjacent to it?

THE PROGRAMME

Any event or function, whatever shape it may take, must have a programme; without one, it is impossible to manage successfully. Also, without a programme, even a simple one, delegates and others attending the event will be confused and frustrated and the objectives of the event will not be achieved, resulting in your appearing unprofessional. Some programmes will, by the nature of the event, be formal; others less so.

THE CHARACTERISTICS AND CATEGORIES OF EVENTS

Annual meetings

Venues will vary, ranging from hotels or public halls to major exhibition halls or conference sites. All should be easily accessible for members and/or shareholders.

Annual meetings will normally be in a formal setting and have a formal agenda, at least for part of the meeting. The adoption of the previous minutes, chairman's address, presentation and adoption of the annual accounts and the appointment of auditors, non-executive directors etc are all items that form the basis of the programme, or agenda, for such meetings.

The amount of prior notice required and the methods to be used to summon an annual general meeting are usually laid down, either within the constitution of the organization or by the terms of a company's legal requirements. Whatever they are they must be strictly adhered to or the meeting could be invalid or declared unconstitutional.

Conferences

Conferences are a good method of direct communication, with many opportunities for good public relations. Below are some hints and guidelines on organizing them, from the public relations point of view (see also Appendix 8).

General characteristics

Conferences normally cover a variety of topics with a common theme. They are a combination of the spoken word (plenary sessions, workshops and 'fringe' activities), audio-visual displays and present-ations, the written word (eg papers delivered), displays and some-times, small trade exhibitions. They tend to be rather impersonal, set in a large hall or theatre, with a platform for the set-piece sessions and speeches.

Conferences can be very sophisticated (eg party political confer-ences), lasting five days and including 'side shows' (eg fringe meetings, talks and receptions) as satellites to the main sessions. Or they can be simple, one-day affairs with a number of set speakers and only 'plenary' or full, formal sessions.

Numbers

Conferences are usually fairly large gatherings. Numbers of delegates can vary from perhaps 150 at the bottom of the scale to several thousand at the top end. The average attendance is usually around the 350–450 mark.

Dates and seasons

Most major conferences tend to be held in the autumn – September through to late October or early November are favourite months. Academic conferences and those held at universities, however, will usually take place during the long summer vacation. This may change in future as some universities are considering scrapping the long vacation and having more semesters in order to become more cost effective.

Duration

Conferences usually last between two and four days, but can sometimes be held for only one day. Weekend conferences are often more favoured by academics and some of the voluntary organizations, while political and major business conferences are usually held during the week and can last up to six days.

Accommodation

Conferences are usually residential and often require a considerable amount of accommodation for delegates. This should be borne in mind when deciding on the venue – availability of hotels and guest houses may be a key factor.

If held at a university, student halls of residence are often used. They are cheaper than hotel accommodation and more plentiful – but much more basic! You must know what kind of accommodation will be expected by your delegates.

Fees and expenses

Delegates to conferences normally pay a fee which may include some extras, but meals, travel and even certain accommodation may not be included in the fee. Guest speakers normally have their travel expenses paid in addition to their fee, unless they waive it. This can all be quite expensive, especially if the keynote speaker lives in Australia!

Travel arrangements

Travel arrangements for conferences need careful planning, particularly for delegates who may not have visited this country before. Most overseas delegates will travel by air, but there may well be rail travel involved as well, for which the conference organizers will be responsible.

Air travel

Special arrangements may have to be made at airports to greet delegates on arrival and dispatch them with onward travel arrangements. If the conference venue is abroad, sometimes a particular airline, usually the 'flag' carrier of the host country (eg QANTAS for Australia), may offer special reduced rates for delegates – but only with that carrier. It is worth checking with the airline.

Rail travel

Some railway companies offer group travel fares, with reduced rates for delegates' rail tickets within the UK. Check with the appropriate companies to confirm whether this service is available (see Appendix 6).

Sponsorship

You may be lucky and get a major sponsor for the whole conference. They will, of course, normally expect their name to appear in 'bright lights' during the conference, and may lay down certain other conditions. Sponsorship can be enormously helpful and, if you are going to get it, you should obviously liaise with the sponsor's PR department.

The speakers

First-class keynote speakers are essential for the major, plenary sessions. They will enhance the programme and help to attract delegates.

Keynote speakers must be chosen with care. Ideally, they should not only be well known but should also have expert knowledge of their subject. They should also be good public speakers. Nothing is worse than having a keynote speaker who, while an expert in the chosen field, is an abysmal speaker. Take advice if necessary.

Presentation equipment

The standard of visual aids and sound equipment can make all the difference between a good conference and a mediocre one. Presentations should ideally be a combination of audio-visual and speech, with well-produced handouts. Make sure, therefore, that there are sufficient visual aids available of good quality, plus back-up for emergencies!

Find out what equipment the speaker intends to use. Have sufficient spare items available such as slide cartridges and carousels for speakers (who may bring their own slides), overhead projection equipment and other visual aid equipment. Check that all the PA and CCTV systems you intend to use are 'online'. Check and double check.

Social programmes

Most conferences will have some kind of a social programme as part of the conference proceedings. These can range from a reception on the first evening, to a series of parties, a full-blown dinner with speeches, an awards presentation, tours and visits, and sometimes a separate programme for delegates' partners. This might be a day trip to a local tourist attraction, a shopping trip or a 'mini' programme lasting for one or two days.

Seminars and workshops

These are usually much smaller gatherings than conferences, with normally only a single topic. Numbers are usually not more than 25–50. Much of the detailed planning required is the same as for conferences – though on a 'micro' rather than a 'macro' scale.

Duration
Seminars and workshops are shorter in duration, lasting usually one day, or at most two. Sometimes they may take place in an evening.

Programme
Whilst a programme is required it will be much simpler in content. Sessions are more informal and are designed to encourage discussion. Workshops tend to break up into still smaller groups and include active participation by those attending.

Venues
Because they are smaller, seminars and workshops are often held at more modest venues than conferences. Hotel suites, lecture halls or other similar sized venues are the norm.

Speakers
Speakers are normally fewer and less prestigious. There will be keynote speakers who address the same subject, but probably from different viewpoints.

Accommodation
Seminars and workshops are not usually residential so accommodation should not present a problem. If it is required, then a hotel venue with appropriate accommodation 'on site' will usually be the answer.

Travel arrangements
Normally, delegates make their own travel arrangements. Delegates may have to pay for their own overnight accommodation or it may be part of the whole package. Keynote speakers may have to be paid and accommodated overnight.

Fees and expenses
Delegates to seminars and workshops normally pay a fee and keynote speakers may have to be paid, though less than for a conference. Overall, expenses will be less.

Equipment

The same rules apply here as for a conference, though on a smaller scale. Many hotels will provide all the equipment necessary for audio-visual presentations and even video and PA equipment. However, check it all out first. It may not be very good, or it may be faulty. And they may charge extra for using it!

12

Visits

All types of visits require a degree of planning and organizing, depending on the nature of the visit and the status of the visitor. Getting all the details right, so that the visit is a success, is one of the principal roles of public relations, be it for a client or in-house for one's own organization. A successful visit can do wonders for the reputation and the image of the organization concerned, by placing it firmly in the public eye and giving it, and often its work, a very high profile. Reputations, however, can be made – and destroyed – by the success or otherwise of a visit.

If the guest of honour is a VIP, such as a member of the Royal Family, a politician, a civic or other dignitary, special considerations may have to be taken into account. Advice on how to handle such visits is given below.

Some general rules will apply to all types of visit, with detailed differences depending on the circumstances. Before any visit you will need to gather as much detailed information as you can so that your planning can begin.

VIP VISITS

Two overriding characteristics of VIP visits are the timetabling that has to be adhered to and, in certain cases, the security measures required. There will also be, inevitably, some level of protocol to be observed. Matters also arise such as who should greet the VIP, how the visitor is to be addressed, what precedence takes place in any procession etc. (See also Appendix 9.)

Foreign VIPs

When foreign VIPs such as ambassadors or diplomats are involved, appropriate liaison and some forward planning is additionally required. You may also need input from local organizations, such as the police and the local authority in the area of the visit, with whom you should liaise over the details of the visit.

Your particular visit may only be one part of a much longer, more widespread visit by the VIP concerned, who may well be going to several other locations in the area or region. Do not forget to alert the Central Office of Information, which may want details of the proposed visit so as to be able to alert appropriate overseas media.

ROYAL VISITS

Here, security is usually the main consideration, and there will be a number of other agencies and organizations who will be involved. These will include either Buckingham Palace or Kensington Palace, the county's Lieutenancy Office and the Lord-Lieutenant, the police and the various mayoral offices at the local town halls. There may be other host organizations with which you should discuss the part they will play in the visit. (For details see Appendix 10.)

13

Sponsorship and educational activities

Sponsorship is really a logical development of the old fashioned patronage. The latter term is still used on occasions, but sponsorship is the term more commonly used today. A patron is described in the dictionary as someone who 'countenances, supports, protects or gives influence to . . . [an individual]'. Sponsorship is described as being 'a business deal which is intended to be to the advantage of both the sponsor and the sponsored . . . a separate element of marketing'. The principle of sponsorship is the same as that of patronage, but it is no longer confined to one person.

PATRONAGE

In the past monarchs, the church and the aristocracy – in other words the rich – both in this country and in Europe, were usually the main patrons. They were benefactors of the arts in general, mostly for philanthropic reasons. For example, the painter Michelangelo was sponsored by the Pope to paint the roof of the Sistine Chapel in Rome, and many other notable European Renaissance painters enjoyed wealthy patronage from the aristocracy and the church.

In this country monarchs have, at various times, sponsored artists, such as van Dyck and Sir Peter Lely, as well as writers and musicians. The composer Handel was frequently sponsored by different members of the aristocracy and royalty, among whom were such notables as the Duke of Chandos and George I, the latter both when he was the Elector of Hanover and later when he became King of England.

SPONSORSHIP

This is the provision of resources (either in cash or kind) for an independent activity, in return for the benefits which it is anticipated will accrue by virtue of that support.

There are many examples of sponsorship today. They range from sponsoring the individual performance of a play, concert or opera, to sponsorship of a Premier League football team for a whole season, a national rugby or cricket team tour, an international sporting fixture, local junior teams or even a local competition of some sort.

Sponsorship today is not only given for altruistic purposes, but also for sound commercial reasons. On the whole, the days of very wealthy individuals who would sponsor a musician, a writer or an artist are long gone; nowadays there are different, and differing, reasons for sponsorship: usually either philanthropic, strictly commercial, or a mixture of both.

Philanthropy

There have been many famous philanthropists in the last one hundred years, both in this country and the USA. They include John D Rockefeller, Dale Carnegie (who founded free libraries in both England and Ireland), Sir Joseph Lever (the soap manufacturer who created the Lever Art Gallery), and George Cadbury (who sponsored adult education and was a pioneer in town planning and the provision of good social housing).

Today, the number of individual philanthropists who will sponsor is small. There are some charitable trusts and foundations that will fund individuals, but they, too, are the exception. The Churchill

Scholarship or the Rhodes Scholarships for individual university students are two examples of a type of modern philanthropy.

Subsidy

Government sponsorship is better described as subsidy (eg the Arts Council). It normally takes the form of financial grant aid towards various activities, mostly in the fields of the performing arts.

Another form of indirect government grant aid is through the National Lottery, with partial funding being made to various causes, both large and small. The National Heritage is yet another form of subsidy, for the preservation of ancient monuments, buildings and similar areas of outstanding national importance.

Endorsement

Another form of sponsorship. This is where money is paid to an organization, or to an individual, in return for which the recipient agrees to use specific items, often clothing or sports equipment, provided by the sponsor. Examples of this are the supply of Land Rover vehicles for a trans-Sahara expedition, or the use of specific clothing and tinned foods on a Mount Everest expedition.

Profile

Not all sponsorship is high profile, spectacular or publicized. Supplies for expeditions or round the world voyages in yachts will often not get the same publicity as, say, a Test cricket series. Sometimes the sponsor prefers not to have a high profile: Cadbury-Schweppes sponsored the hugely successful Children's Art Competition every year for a considerable period, but with a comparatively low profile; little publicity or press coverage being given to it outside schools. Yet it attracted huge numbers of entries, both from individual children and schools, and was very popular.

WHY SPONSOR?

Why, then, do firms or organizations get involved in sponsorship? It may be simply a genuine desire to make an activity financially viable (eg Royal Insurance and the Royal Shakespeare Company), or it may offer a number of good opportunities to test new components (motor racing, yacht racing). Sponsors must know why they want to sponsor, and evaluate carefully all proposals for sponsorship they receive. The proposals must show tangible objectives before a decision is made to get involved.

Commercial reasons

Industry and government are now the principal sponsors in the areas of the arts, recreation, sport and leisure. Today most sport, the performing arts and many other cultural pursuits are almost entirely reliant on gaining sponsorship – from whatever source they can – to enable them to continue their activities.

Usually the overriding reason for sponsorship is the ability, through the sponsorship, to be able to communicate the name of the firm, product or organization to a huge audience, and to do so repeatedly. A good example of this is Cadbury's sponsorship of Granada Television's *Coronation Street*, which is worth £10m per year – one of the largest ever TV sponsorships.

It can also be good public relations for a company to be seen to be supporting a particular activity.

Familiarity and goodwill

Sponsorship achieves familiarity through repetition of association and the impact this can have. It exploits the psychology that we tend to prefer products and organizations that we know. It also generates goodwill, the 'feel-good factor', since the sponsor is seen to be generous, gives pleasure and interest to many people, and will therefore be more highly regarded. This can have a beneficial 'spin-off' effect on that organization's products or the services it provides.

FORMS OF SPONSORSHIP

Let us consider some of the several different forms that sponsorship can take.

Books and publications

This type of sponsorship can take the form of either:

- A business proposition, where the book is wholly sponsored for publication, eg *Shell Guides to the Countryside, The Guinness Book of Records, Michelin Guides.*
- A joint publication. In this case the publisher prints and produces the book; production and distribution costs are then shared between the sponsor and the publisher. The publisher can sell the book, the sponsor can give it away. An example of this was *The Power of Speech – A History of STC 1883–1983*, published by Allen & Unwin for Standard Telephone & Cable Company.

Exhibitions and events

These are often sponsored by trade associations, publishers, commercial organizations or professional associations. Usually they are a blend of public relations and business initiatives. Examples are:

- the *Daily Mail*: Ideal Home Exhibition;
- Society of Motor Manufacturers and Traders: the Motor Show;
- the Royal Agricultural Society: the Royal Show;
- the *Evening Standard*: BAFTA Awards.

Arts and culture

The arts have always depended on patronage. Government subsidy under the patronage of the Arts Council is never sufficient, so sponsorship, either for a season, for an individual performance or of an exhibition, is now becoming accepted as the norm.

Causes and charities

There can be times when it is of mutual benefit for industry to sponsor a charity or a given good cause. This may be as simple as donating a proportion of the selling price of a product to the charity, or it could be sponsoring a video or paying for advertising space.

Expeditions and special activities

Explorations, mountain climbing expeditions – outdoor feats of endurance of any sort are usually very costly to equip and carry out. They rely on either financial support or support in 'kind' in the form of food, clothing or equipment. In return for providing this, the sponsor will receive some publicity, plus any additional research and development benefits from having new items of equipment thoroughly tried and tested under 'field' conditions.

Sport

This is the largest area of activity in sponsorship, and it has become a very big part of business practice. It is a growth area, with more and more sports being included. In many cases, sponsorship is from several firms or organizations, some providing the sponsorship in kind, others with money.

In motor racing, both the cars and their drivers have effectively become advertisement 'hoardings' for a range of motor sport related products. Football strips often display sponsors' logos and product brand names.

Local events

National companies with local branches may sponsor a local or regional event, a flower show, carnival or similar event. This can also cover some unusual sporting events, such as archery or fly casting, at country fairs.

Professional awards

These are usually long-established awards for either individuals or organizations, or both. Examples include awards to the media, such as the *photographer, journalist or newspaper of the year*, and show-business awards such as the *Evening Standard* awards and the *BAFTAs*.

Public service and civic awards

Such sponsorship is made in the public interest, by local authorities, local residents or the business community. Examples include sponsoring litter-bins, the 'greening' of an urban area or hanging flower baskets on lamp posts.

Educational activities

As well as patronizing education, sponsorship may also be an investment in training and recruitment. New 'chairs' at universities are often only made possible because of a sponsor from industry. Many firms endow travelling scholarships, exhibitions, bursaries, research fellowships etc, relative to their industries. A recent example of this type of sponsorship was the research work carried out at the University of Warwick for Jaguar Cars Ltd, related to the design of the proposed new 'small' Jaguar car.

Other firms may donate appropriate equipment, or even whole rooms furnished and equipped, to colleges and schools; or present trophies, prizes or other awards to successful students.

THE NATIONAL LOTTERY

This could be described as a new form of sponsorship, though in a category of its own. It could also be described as a form of subsidy, or even patronage.

It is probably too early to say what overall effects the National Lottery may have on sponsorship as a whole in the long term. There is no doubt, however, that it is already having an impact on some forms of commercial sponsorship, on donations to charities, to the performing arts, some cultural activities, and even some aspects of sport.

The best use of monies generated by the National Lottery in the future is an issue being debated at many levels, including the present government.

EVALUATION

When any sponsorship has been undertaken – in whatever shape or form – evaluation needs to be carried out so as to measure how effective the sponsorship was, in terms of both the sponsor and the sponsored. Evaluation can be done in a number of ways, all of which are dealt with in Chapter 19. However, it is very important that the value of any such operations can be fairly and accurately judged for their effectiveness.

14

Business writing

GENERAL RULES

Good writing technique is essential to all who work in public relations. Not only is it important to have reasonably legible handwriting and correct spelling, but the ability to express oneself clearly and easily on paper shows a professional approach to one's work. The latter is of course essential when it comes to writing feature articles for publication.

Clear, logically argued, succinctly written and costed reports, proposals, letters and memoranda are all necessary in order to spell out clearly the writer's recommendations. It is not only businesslike but shows the writer to be capable of logical, responsible thought.

When writing anything, two considerations must be taken into account:

1. The reader – often a busy person, who will therefore probably only 'scan' read the work and will need to be given any main points and recommendations clearly so that they can be assimilated quickly.
2. The publication – any article, paper or publication should always be logical in its flow, capable of easy reference by the reader and be jargon free.

REPORTS AND PROPOSALS

Reports and proposals should always be clear and precise, objective and well thought out. It is little use making verbal recommendations only; they should always be backed up by a written report. When a report is well presented, well thought through and properly costed, it is much easier to argue your case successfully. (See Appendix 11.)

Do your homework and research first, and make sure that you are factual. Back up any proposals with facts and figures.

MEMORANDA

These are the most common way for organizations to communicate internally, closely followed nowadays by e-mail. Memos, like reports, should be clear, succinct, factual, easily understood and *brief*. Copies can be sent to third parties and others if appropriate, for their information or action. Memos should not be long. If they look like becoming too long, then a full report may be more appropriate. Memos are sometimes handwritten (but see 'House styles' below).

House styles

Organizations usually have their own quite distinctive 'house styles' for all written work. Sometimes this can be very specific, down to the type, colour, weight and make of paper to be used; the font, typeface size and the detailed layout of all correspondence, from memos to papers, invoices, reports and letters. The amount of detail varies from organization to organization. Usually there are manuals that can be consulted.

MINUTES

It sometimes falls to us to have to act as minute takers at meetings. Everyone has their own way of doing this. Minute taking is almost an art form and requires lots of practice. Below are some tips borne out of experience – the hard way – by the author over many years. (See also Appendices 12, 13 and 14.)

The production of minutes

It is advisable to write up the rough hand-written minutes into their formal style as soon as possible after the meeting, preferably within 24 hours, while they are still fresh in your mind. Send the proofed draft direct to the Chair of the committee, or whoever presided at the meeting, for their approval before general circulation. This is the correct 'protocol' and saves any embarrassment later.

Note taking

A hardback, A4-sized book for writing the minutes in is useful. It saves using scrappy bits of paper and can be referred to later, especially if the agendas are pasted in on the left-hand page and the minutes hand-written on the right-hand page. Minutes are not normally taken verbatim, unlike court reporting. They should include the names of all keynote speakers.

Style

There will be certain house rules to follow and special procedures may have to be observed. Check previous minutes for style and content as well as detail – they will tell you a great deal.

FEATURE ARTICLES

This is a quite different sort of writing. Remember, a feature article is *not* a long news release. It has an entirely different literary style and form of its own, with its own special characteristics, uses and values. Whereas a news release is given wide distribution, an article goes to one journal for one edition and, if well written, is unlikely to be edited. A feature article is normally written exclusively for one publication and cannot be reproduced elsewhere without permission. However, an article can be rewritten in a different way using the same basic information, and can then be published in other magazines, journals etc. Each article will be exclusive to that publication.

Feature articles do take time to prepare, research and write. Negotiations with editors, obtaining the necessary permission from others, checking drafts and preparing artwork are all time consuming.

The advantages

Feature articles nonetheless have certain advantages. Journals and magazines containing such articles are often kept in binders or in libraries. The articles themselves are often considered to be authoritative, especially if the author is an acknowledged expert or authority on the particular topic: they are therefore frequently kept as reference material, as part of the literature on the subject, and reprints can be made for circulation. Finally, they are informative and usually well illustrated.

How to write an article

There is no magic formula for this, but there are two hints that may be helpful:

1.   The theme – there must be a theme, idea or subject, not just a bare description. This theme should persuade the editor of the publication concerned that the article should be published.
2.   Permission – you must be able to get access to the information needed to write the article. Permission may have to be obtained from the appropriate people – approaches are usually best made through the public relations officer (if there is one) or directly to those concerned.

Once this has been settled, approach the editor. *Never write speculative articles, because you do not know what is wanted, who will publish it or even who will read it.*

Writing the article

Who writes a public relations article depends on the publication for which it is being written. Some insist on using their own staff writers, others use freelance writers, or prefer the proposer to write it for them.

Staff writers
If the article is to be written by someone working for the publication, you can supply the ideas and facilities and arrange interviews, photography etc. They actually write the article in-house. Good –

because it has the independent authority of the by-lined staff writer. Bad – because the loss of control and possible bias.

A contributor

This is normally a freelance professional writer. Again, you supply the theme, ideas and facilities. They write the article.

Others

There are a number of different options here. Depending on the subject matter, the subject of the article and various other factors, it could be one of the following:

- an in-house public relations officer – about his or her organization;
- a public relations consultant – on behalf of the client's firm, product or organization;
- a freelance writer – to get an outside viewpoint;
- a personality – a famous person, or a well-known media or other personality;
- a 'ghost' writer – sometimes used where the subject is not particularly articulate or literary.

Proposing the article

Having thought out your ideas, and having worked out the preliminaries, it is time to get in touch with the editor of the publication in which you will publish the article. Having aroused their interest with a letter or telephone call the proposal can then be sent. This should always include:

- the idea (the theme);
- any clearances obtained, or to be obtained, for permission to publish;
- any clearance for research.

If the publisher is enthusiastic about your ideas and commissions the article then you will require the following information from them:

- How many words should it be?
- Is any special treatment needed?

- How many and what type of illustrations are required?
- What is the issue date of the publication?
- What are the copy dates/deadlines?

Commercial references

These should always be kept to a minimum. A feature article should not be accused of being an 'advertorial'.

Fees

Normally there are no fees payable for writing feature articles, as they are written in the employer's time, on the employer's paper. However, fees may be payable in the case of an independent consultant who is commissioned to write an article by a publication.

Agreements

The normal agreement is to publish 'subject to sight of copy'. In other words, the editor has discretion as to whether to publish, depending on the final article.

Writing the article

This is probably the most difficult part. It is worthwhile setting out on paper first the rough way in which the article is to be written, as a guide. The Frank Jefkins 'Seven-point Model for Feature Articles' is recommended as being straightforward and easy to remember. Given below, are points that could be used when writing an article about the introduction of a new piece of technical equipment:

- the opening paragraph – the beginning – should lead into the body of the article;
- the previous or present situation – and any related problems;
- the search for a solution – the 'meat' of the article;
- the solution and results achieved – how it was done;
- the closing paragraph – with a summary and, possibly, a 'look ahead'.

Having written the draft, check it with any sources of information, as it may have to be amended. Work back from the deadline or copy date.

Reference books

It is worthwhile having a few aids to writing: *Roget's Thesaurus*, a dictionary of quotations, the *Oxford English Dictionary* and a copy of *Fowler's English Usage* are a good basis from which to start. You can add any other suitable, specialist books as appropriate.

Conclusion

A good feature article, well written and illustrated, is an excellent form of public relations, and can benefit the organization featured, its products and its business generally. It also can benefit you, as the author.

15

Crisis management

'Crisis public relations', or 'crisis management' as it is often called, is a form of public relations which until comparatively recently was little known about or even thought of. However, in recent years the number and scale of disasters has highlighted the need for a particular form of public relations that enables an organization to cope with a crisis situation whatever form it may take, and come out of it with some credibility. This chapter takes a brief look at some aspects of crisis and how to plan for them, with a checklist of things to remember if the worst occurs (see Appendix 15).

Lack of crisis management or planning can have a devastating effect on an organization's image, its credibility, its reputation, and on the morale of its employees; whether it is the government of a country, a multinational corporation or a small company. Because very often the organization is not seen to be in a 'high risk' business in the strictest sense does not mean that there will never be an occasion when it will not experience an emergency of some sort. It is well to be prepared.

WHAT IS CRISIS MANAGEMENT?

Crisis management is the ability to cope with any emergency situation that may arise in such a way that the minimum amount of 'damage' is caused to the organization – in whatever context that may be. Any organization that has the misfortune to experience an emergency situation, of any sort, must not only be able to cope, but must be seen to be able to do so. Otherwise it will suffer damage, in terms both of its image and its credibility, not only with its own workforce but also with the public.

HOW TO COPE

Often the first reaction to a crisis situation is one of panic, followed by confusion. Certainly, the first stages of any crisis situation are usually ones of apparent chaos. Information is at best vague or more likely non-existent. Rumours abound, whipped up by the media in search of a good news story. If it is a situation where there has been loss of life (a major explosion, or a fire) there will be additional problems of trying to find out who is missing and informing friends and relatives.

An enormous volume and variety of detail has to be dealt with quickly, calmly and efficiently. Just how does one cope? Knowing *how* to deal with such a situation, and then dealing with it well, is the key. It can be done, and done in such a way as to turn the situation to your advantage; at the very least to limit any damage to a minimum.

What follows are some of the basic rules that apply whatever form a crisis may take and if you follow them you will be prepared. Obviously details will vary with each situation, but the principles remain the same. These, then, form the infrastructure, or skeleton, for the management of a crisis situation.

Assess

Look at your organization as objectively as possible. Try and imagine a situation that could arise: a major explosion in a factory, an outbreak of food poisoning, a bomb at a mainline railway terminus, a fire in a shopping precinct. These are the sorts of scenarios that could affect

Crisis management: Establish crisis centre

your organization and its reputation. Think of it as the 'What if. . .' situation.

Plan

Draw up contingency plans, however simple, to cover different possible scenarios. Each plan may have to be different, but it may be that one plan can be adapted to suit all potential crises.

Prepare

Earmark suitable premises as a crisis operations centre and appoint key staff; allocate their tasks and responsibilities. Good communications are vital in any crisis situation, so look at what communications facilities you have available. Decide what else you will need. Dedicate separate direct telephone lines and equipment before the crisis occurs.

Train

Practise with all those involved in the team so that they become familiar with what they have to do, when, and how. Quick response is critical in the early stages of any crisis. Train and train again.

Modify

No plan will last forever. Situations, people, circumstances all change. Therefore remember to update or modify your plan at regular intervals to meet these changes.

AFTER IT IS OVER

The aftermath of a crisis can sometimes be messy and protracted. There is often much to be cleared up, both figuratively and literally. The life and work of your crisis team may have to be extended, albeit in a different form, to cope with it all. There will also most likely be a complicated and lengthy inquiry, with evidence to be collected, all of which will involve much work by the organization – and your team members.

Careful and skilful handling of all the public relations issues involved can considerably lessen any lingering stigma and false impressions that may have been created.

16

Working with the media

The media, or broadcast media as it is usually called, is different from the press. It has special advantages and disadvantages. Radio and television have one thing in common: they are both transient unless recorded, unlike newspapers which can be read again and again. The content of newspapers may date very quickly (yesterday's news is history), but they can be stored and retrieved at will. Properly used, the media can be extremely valuable in public relations terms, in getting particular messages across to a wide audience, provided that its special attributes are understood.

IMPACT

There is a lot more to broadcasting and the role for public relations in the media than merely sending news releases to radio and television stations. It must be remembered that, unlike the printed word, broadcast messages are somewhat difficult to retain. However, they do have an instant impact, eg a natural disaster such as an earthquake. But because of their transience, broadcast messages can often be misunderstood or quickly forgotten.

AUDIENCES

Television and radio have huge audiences, even bigger than before with the advent of satellite communication. For instance, CNN news is seen by hundreds of millions of people all over the world today, thanks to the use of satellite broadcasting techniques and equipment. For many years the BBC's World Service has broadcast to millions of listeners in all parts of the world, in their own language as well as in English, and it is still very popular today.

In the UK alone network television attracts up to 40 million viewers, more than 25 per cent greater than the combined total readership of all our national daily papers.

TELEVISION

In recent years the impact that television can have as a medium has increased enormously. Due to increasing use of satellite communication, advanced technology, the introduction of new channels, nationally and internationally in different forms, television coverage worldwide on a 24-hour basis is now possible. Particularly in the case of news bulletins and 'breaking news', response times have been dramatically reduced.

Thus, during times of international crises, it is possible for live television reports to be beamed directly onto national networks continuously, making coverage much more immediate and flexible. Because of this, it also can have a much greater impact on the viewers than was possible in the past.

There are some major characteristics about television that should be remembered:

- Some programmes are still broadcast live, but most are pre-recorded.
- Some programmes are made months in advance of transmission.
- Material can be 'held over' for future use.

Opportunities for coverage using television

News bulletins National and regional.

Magazine programmes Regular features. Open to material that is both topical and of interest to particular groups (eg motorists, farmers, businessmen).

Chat shows/interviews and discussions Participation by personalities, especially if their subjects are interesting.

Serials and soap operas Subjects of public concern and interest can be worked into these in a fictional setting: drugs in *EastEnders*, marriage problems, adoption and transplant ethics in *Coronation Street*, various topical crime issues in *The Bill*, farming topics on *Country File*.

Current affairs programmes Can be very useful to put over major issues. May require cooperation from the public relations practitioner in covering the subject matter, or may be interested in a proposed topic.

Series Material may be produced well in advance and appear at regular intervals.

Library shots External shots may be borrowed or hired: landmarks, special locations etc.

Archival material Film, video or 'still' photos inserted into the programme as background material for scene setting. Fees may be payable.

Properties Properties and materials used in television films are usually credited at the end.

Products	These are not credited, but have nonetheless been seen by viewers.
Stills	Slides and pictures are often used for rostrum camera work on programmes.
Prizes	The 'give-aways' on quiz shows. If recognizable, they can be useful in public relations to propose their use to the producer.

- Editing can break up a sequence or alter the meaning.
- Planning requirements for programme making are demanding (research, locations, lighting, equipment and engineering).

Public relations practitioners must be aware of and understand these technicalities and characteristics.

The down side

Be aware also of some of the pitfalls. Television is often used to amuse and entertain, rather than to inform its audience. So, care and consideration when planning television work is important. Make sure that the right type of programme is selected. Do not use television just because of the glamour associated with the medium – vanity can prove costly and damaging!

Documentary file material

You may have film, video or still material that is of interest, which could be shown in full or in part. Acknowledgements are given and royalty fees paid. The latter are usually negotiable.

Fees and rates

The rate for fees and royalties varies, but are normally negotiated at a rate per minute or part thereof. This will differ depending on where the programme is to be shown, but as an example:

- UK only: £200 per minute or part thereof.
- International distribution: £400 per minute or part thereof.

RADIO

One of the great advantages of radio over television is that it is not confined to indoor audiences. It is a highly portable medium, particularly since the advent of the 'Walkman' belt-portable radios, the clockwork powered radio and other very small portables. For this and other reasons it is less restrictive than television. It is also more adaptable and quicker to produce, requiring fewer facilities.

The radio does not require an immobile audience. It can be listened to whilst doing other things, is often used as a background companion for the elderly, the housebound or for blind people, and is usually better for music programmes as it can be listened to continuously.

It is also more responsive than television. It can broadcast matters such as local road conditions, weather warnings or emergency announcements very quickly. Local radio can cover local areas, and issues, much more effectively and intimately than even regional television.

TELETEXT AND CEEFAX

These are extensions to television available to those whose sets have the facilities to receive them (ie most households). They are effectively a 'visual' magazine programme, covering a wide variety of different topics and giving information which the viewer can call up at will. Teletext and Ceefax are the two principal channels available on terrestrial TV at present in the UK but, with the advent of cable television and satellite television, more are becoming available.

They cover a variety of topics, such as the weather, stock exchange prices, traffic conditions, sports results, news, entertainment, shopping prices, farming prices and travel booking opportunities. Currently, both are being updated, modernized and made easier and more attractive to use, with some visual aids.

Opportunities for coverage using radio

News bulletins   National, regional and local news coverage.

Taped interviews   Done in several ways. The station may commission an interview, or it can be made by the company and supplied to the stations. If the latter, no commercial references should be made during the interview but the company name will normally be given at the start and the finish.

Studio interviews, discussions, talks   Interesting people, conversationalists, commentators and interesting voices are all good potential radio material.

The 'phone-in'   Much used on local radio and increasingly popular. Can be done 'down-the-line' from the office or the home.

Serials, series, soap operas   Public relations messages can be put over on these programmes as with TV. *The Archers*, for example, often carries important messages about farming and related agricultural matters.

TELEVISION NEWS RELEASE LIMITED (TNR)

TNR provides a range of broadcast services for corporate communications. It can supply TV news releases for a variety of organizations, be they commercial companies, charities or other organizations. TNR can also advise on matters such as TV communication strategy, pre-production, filming, editing and distribution of footage to all relevant broadcasters, either in the UK or internationally.

TNR also provides such items as radio news releases, corporate videos for promotional or presentational purposes and media training as well as a whole range of marketing and communication services.

17

External media support

There are often occasions when some form of external assistance may be appropriate to help in the communication and distribution of information for a campaign, or some media activity, to get a message across to the appropriate audience. There are a number of organizations that can help you in this way. They are the UK news agencies who provide a whole range of specific, different types of service depending on your requirements.

There are two main news agencies operating in the UK providing the media in this country and worldwide, both with a centralized news service. They are the Press Association and Reuters. Their unique position at the hub of the media industry enables them to provide support for any media-based activities or for marketing campaigns that you may be involved in. They can help because they know specifically what information the media want and, more importantly, how they like to get it.

DISTRIBUTION

The press release and picture distribution services within these agencies enable you to send messages and images straight into the newsrooms of the UK's media and also to media overseas.

Additionally, there are other methods of distribution using the Internet. The Press Association has two: PA Mediapoint (www.pamediapoint-pr.press.net) and PA Picselect (www.papicselect.com). These two services release press releases or download images placed by customers. They can also host 'virtual pressrooms' complete with text, audio and video clips as well as pictures. They have facilities to produce high quality promotional features, newspaper supplements, magazines and media bulletins on almost any subject to assist your media campaign. Reuters has similar services available upon enquiry.

These press agencies distribute press releases directly into editorial newsrooms, using the same satellite links and lines as its editorial. This means that news releases can be seen simultaneously on thousands of editorial screens across the UK. Every daily national and regional newspaper, national and regional television and radio broadcasting station uses this facility which means that your release could get very extensive coverage.

BROADCAST MEDIA

Similarly, camera crews can be hired to film corporate events and distribute footage to the media and they may have TV and radio studios available in which to conduct live interviews that can then be linked to any worldwide broadcasting system.

MONITORING AND EVALUATION

News agencies monitor the media all the time, thus providing a further tool for public relations activities. The agency's clients and subscribers are able to receive stories at the same time as the UK newsrooms, keeping them one step ahead of the headlines. Similarly, there are e-mail services supplying details of events for the forthcoming 24 hours that are likely to make the news during that period.

This can be particularly important at times of 'breaking news' and also be useful when it comes to evaluating the level of coverage received and thus the success of a campaign.

EDITORIAL SUPPORT

Other means of assistance can be found through a variety of editorial support services operated by these agencies, such as a centralized copy-taking and transcription service. This service can be used to help with some of your routine day-to-day activities, letting you concentrate on other activities and core business.

This service means that news agencies can take copy and put it directly into an editorial system. Whatever that item may be, whether a feature or a piece of breaking news, it enables stories to be sent to newsrooms quickly and accurately at all times. This service will enable you to do likewise.

News agencies can also provide press lists appropriate to your needs.

INTEGRATED SERVICES DIGITAL NETWORK

Integrated Services Digital Network (ISDN) is a digital telephone exchange line system introduced by BT (which will supply further information on request). Conforming to international standards, it can be used anywhere in the UK and around the globe, from Europe to the Pacific Rim, the USA and Australia.

How does it work?

ISDN is a digital telephone line, but much more powerful than the present ones. It works through the public network, while achieving the speed and clarity of a private network. At present it comes in two forms:

1. ISDN 2 – the Basic Rate Service, designed to meet the needs of smaller businesses, or parts of larger organizations.
2. ISDN 30 – the Primary Rate Service. This can meet requirements of both large and small companies or locations.

Using ISDN

ISDN will allow you to send and receive any amount of information in a variety of forms, such as voice, data, images and videos. It can be used to make phone calls, send large amounts of data around the country, rush photographs and artwork to the advertising agency or hold video conferences. As it is a public network service you only pay for what you use and you achieve greater cost savings as it allows for fast call set-up and then takes a fraction of the time to send the information.

Several large businesses in the UK, such as Bass Brewers, have installed this system, enabling them to gain a competitive edge in the brewing industry, halving packaging lead times with their design data delivery and for desktop conferencing facilities.

MORE INFORMATION

For further details of the range of the various services that news agencies have to offer, in the first instance you can contact either:

The Press Association Limited
Tel: (0207) 963 7000
Fax: (0207) 963 7090
e-mail: information@pa.press.net
Web site: www.pa.press.net

or:

Reuters
Tel: (0207) 250 1122
Fax: (0207) 542 7921
You can visit their Web sites at either: www.reuters.co.uk
or for worldwide coverage: www.reuters.com
e-mail for UK coverage:
press releases: uk.general.news@reuters.com
pictures: lon.pictures@reuters.com

18

Planning and programming

WHY HAVE A PROGRAMME?

Unless there is a programme for public relations work it will tend to become muddled, disjointed and little of it will be completed satisfactorily; nor can the results of unplanned work be analysed successfully. A public relations programme is not about short-term, reactive or haphazard public relations.

Part of the IPR definition of public relations includes the following: 'the deliberate, planned and sustained effort to establish and maintain mutual understanding between an organization and its publics'.

The essentials to remember when planning are:

- 'the deliberate, planned and sustained effort';
- 'establish and maintain';
- 'mutual understanding'.

These are the concepts. Public relations programmes should be planned using them as descriptives so as to achieve the best, definitive results.

THE PROGRAMME

A programme should be designed to last for a reasonable length of time, at least 12 months, if not longer. Any such programme is a complex undertaking, and should cover the strategy for public relations activity. Thus, the programme is the 'strategy' and, within it, the individual events or activities are the 'tactics'. When planning public relations programmes, there are various points to be borne in mind.

The unpredictable

Any programme should be planned well in advance, certainly not less than about three months. Allowances must always be made for the unexpected or the unpredictable (otherwise known as Murphy's Law). Often things will happen simultaneously. *Never* try to operate on a day-to-day basis.

Flexibility

Build in flexibility and allow for regular reviews at stated intervals. Also, allow for certain 'fixed feasts' – these are events that happen regularly, eg publishing house journals, annual reports, launches, exhibitions etc.

Priorities

In order to achieve the best results for the programme, always take into account the following resources (or lack of them):

● the necessary human resources;
● material resources;
● financial resources.

There will inevitably be constraints, and therefore priorities have to be worked out in advance.

Budgets

In-house public relations departments have to present a costed programme to management. Similarly, a consultancy making a presentation to a client must include a detailed programme of the proposals, supported by a fully calculated budget. This will enable the client to know exactly what can be expected for the money, and the consultancy will know how much it can expect to get paid!

Controlling the programme

The best control is to use a simple daily or weekly system. There may be an existing system that can be adapted quickly and easily. Below are two examples of methods of control.

Time sheets
These provide a simple check on how much time – and human resource – is being spent. They can act as an early warning system for any 'overruns' that may occur, and can also be used as a 'benchmark' for any future work. They also help in calculating fees. A secretariat can collect and then collate time sheets, keep running totals and compare them with any 'target' totals.

Job numbers
These are useful for controlling costs by identifying all related invoices and orders. Job numbers help to isolate and identify items for subsequent allocation to cost centres.

HOW TO PLAN THE PROGRAMME

To be successful, the plan should be systematic. A good way of achieving this is to use the 'six-point' method devised by the late Frank Jefkins, as set out below:

1. appreciation of the situation;
2. setting of objectives;
3. definition of your publics;
4. selection of the media;
5. budgets;
6. assessment of results.

Remember:

- the identified publics must relate to the objectives;
- the media and the techniques used will be the means of communicating with the public;
- to consider any budget constraints when drawing up the plan; they will affect:
    - the number of objectives;
    - the identified publics;
    - availability of the media;
    - types of media to be used.

The end result of your planning will be the programme or proposition.

19

Assessment and evaluation

ASSESSMENT

At various times in life goals have to be set and objectives met, if only for the purpose of personal achievement. Some sort of assessment then has to take place to see if all (or even any) of your objectives have been met, and whether what had been planned has been effectively carried out.

It will be recalled that in the last chapter, when looking at public relations programming and planning, one of the key factors in the six point plan was 'setting of objectives': *'We cannot successfully plan without objectives, and without those objectives we cannot assess results.'*

In public relations terms, unless objectives are set and some form of assessment and subsequent evaluation carried out, it is impossible to say whether those objectives have been achieved, how effective that particular programme has been or, for that matter, how successful any public relations work has been. Without objectives there can be no assessment, which, along with evaluation, are of paramount importance in public relations work. Assessment and evaluation show how effective, objective and purposeful a particular piece of work is, or has been, in achieving the objectives that were set. If management knows what it wants from public relations it will expect it to be work that produces results that can be measured.

Enlightened management, in organizations such as Marks & Spencer, use this sort of measurable public relations as a business technique. They do not spend a great deal on advertising, but have good public relations and an excellent reputation.

EVALUATION

There are three main ways to evaluate the results of a public relations programme:

1. observation and experience;
2. feedback and analysis;
3. research.

Observation and experience

This method is probably the crudest and simplest, but it is also the least expensive form of evaluation. It is not, perhaps, the most scientific method, but can be very effective. It is similar to a military intelligence-gathering operation, in that it draws on a variety of sources of 'raw' information and material from which certain conclusions are then made.

However, it may also be somewhat subjective, in that the analysts may draw incorrect or biased conclusions based on insufficient evidence, either qualitative or quantitative. Nevertheless, if other means are not available, then it should be used. Examples of this method are:

- *A community relations programme.* The success or otherwise of this programme could be measured by monitoring the attitude of the local media, before, during and after the programme. Also by observing the local community, through conversations, correspondence and even their participation at public events dealing with matters affecting them.
- *A recruitment campaign* (to raise the standard of the calibre of staff being recruited). By analysing all the job application forms for

posts in the organization over a given period, a view can be taken as to whether or not the campaign was effective.

- *A media relations campaign*. Was it successful? Did it produce more qualitative as well as quantitative press coverage? By collating all press cuttings, media tapes and any other coverage, the success or otherwise of the programme can be 'measured' and certain conclusions drawn from the results.

Feedback and analysis

Public relations is a two-way process, so it should be listening as well as telling. Feedback, and the subsequent analysis of the information received, can be a very useful method of assessing the effectiveness of work carried out.

Again, it is a form of intelligence gathering, or detective work, in that a mass of 'raw' material has to be collected together in different forms, sifted through, collated, kept or discarded, and then analysed. Out of that analysis should emerge a picture that will give an accurate assessment of the effectiveness of the programme – a sort of 'jigsaw'.

Feedback can also be somewhat subjective. There is a danger of this unless the analysts ensure that they are not being selective over what they retain – perhaps for political reasons. All relevant information should be retained for analysis, however insignificant it may appear. Analysts should take everything into account when assessing information and in their subsequent analysis – again, the detective work analogy. Feedback will come from a wide variety of sources, both internal and external, such as:

- complaints;
- ideas and suggestions;
- reports and recommendations;
- newspaper cuttings – whether qualitative or quantitative;
- broadcast media monitoring (as above);
- books, articles and features;
- parliamentary and local authority committee reports;
- minutes and notes of meetings;
- conversations – the least accurate but sometimes indicative.

Analysis

The analyst (that is, the PRO) then has to examine all the material collected, analysing and classifying it so that a report can be drawn up and presented to management.

A 'source' rating, or system of categorization for reliability and accuracy, may be helpful. This system, say ranging from category 'A' being the most reliable, through to 'F' being the least accurate, or reliable, may be the most straightforward and appropriate.

In most cases assessment may not require such a complicated or sophisticated system, but it is better to use a systematic approach rather than carry out assessments haphazardly.

Based on the results of the analysis, the PRO can then make the necessary assessment and produce his or her report.

Action

The PRO then has to advise management of the results and what action should be taken, for example some form of pre-emptive action. The results of the analysis may have to be acted upon immediately, or may merely be filed for future reference.

Research

The third (and probably the most objective and scientific) means of evaluation and assessment in use today is research. Market research is probably the most-used method in this area of public relations, and issued to assist in:

- changing attitudes;
- improving awareness;
- altering images.

With the research method of assessment, before any programme is carried out there has to be some initial research to establish a starting point. This creates a 'snapshot' of the present position, the base-line from which to work.

Pre-programme research

There are two main ways of conducting this base-line or pre-pro-gramme research: first, by independent primary research; second, by using an existing 'omnibus' survey with a special questionnaire insert.

Interim research

Following completion of this market research, objectives can be identified and drawn up for implementation in the programme. Progress can be monitored throughout the programme by having interim surveys at stated intervals if this is thought necessary or appropriate. They could be helpful if the programme is a long-term one, as they will indicate whether the programme is targeted correctly, is having any impact, or is skewed.

Post-programme research

On completion of the programme the follow-up or post-programme research is carried out. A survey after completion should reveal how effective the programme has been.

CONCLUSION

Management can only expect to get properly assessed and evaluated results if they give support to a properly planned and executed programme. Trying to carry out public relations programmes on the cheap will only end up with unassessable results. In public relations terms this is both unacceptable and unprofessional.

For further reading on this subject, see *Planning and Managing a Public Relations Campaign*, Anne Gregory, published by Kogan Page.

20

Conclusion

The many changes in attitudes that have taken place in our society in recent years, with an increasing demand for information, the questioning of decision making and the increasingly voracious appetite for more and more detail about everything that happens, all demonstrate clearly the significant role to be played by public relations and the need for it to provide this information. These changes, together with ever-increasing pressure from the media and the public, in almost every field of activity, also demonstrate the need for effective public relations, to help in changing attitudes, influencing opinion and creating awareness in many different ways.

Public relations is not an exact science, but covers all fields of activity. Its practitioners require a wide range of skills and personal qualities, including sound judgement, integrity, knowledge, organizational skills and personality. Armed with these they will have the ability to communicate, to create knowledge and understanding of events, issues and even individuals. All are essential in the world today. To paraphrase Professor Sam Black, there are two worlds in public relations: one is the practitioner who practises public relations for the benefit of the client or the employer; the other is the very wide range of activities which go to make up public relations practice.

It is all the more important, therefore, that all who work in public relations are not only conversant with all the different activities and techniques, but also keep up to date with all the changes that are taking place in this area of work. The aim of this book has been to try and pass on some of the author's experience, as well as some of the skills and knowledge that are part of public relations, in an easily assimilated way. It is to be hoped that it will help the reader to improve his or her own skills and knowledge.

Further reading

Further, more detailed information on the various topics mentioned in this book can be obtained from books, guidelines, case studies and recommended practice papers. Many of these are available from the Institute of Public Relations, leading bookshops or direct from the publishers. A recommended reading list is also available from the IPR on application. It includes the following titles (among many others):

GENERAL TITLES

Introduction to Public Relations, Sam Black, Modino Press
The Practice of Public Relations (4th edn), Sam Black, Butterworth Heinemann
How to Manage Public Relations, Norman Stone, McGraw-Hill
Public Relations (4th edn), Frank Jefkins, Pitman
Teach Yourself Public Relations, H & P Lloyd, Hodder & Stoughton
'PR in Practice' Series, edited by Anne Gregory: *Public Relations in Practice; Effective Media Relations; Planning and Managing a Public Relations Campaign; Risk Issue and Crisis Management*, Kogan Page

IPR GUIDELINES

Public Relations and the Law; Public Relations Practice: Its Role and Parameters; Resolving the Advertising/Editorial Conflict; The Use, Misuse and Abuse of Embargoes; Fees and Methods of Charging for Public Relations Services; The News Release; Photographs accompanying News Release Press Kits.

Copies of the guidelines can be obtained from:
The Institute of Public Relations
The Old Trading House
15 Northburgh Street
London EC1V 0PR.

LAW TITLES

Writers' & Artists' Yearbook, Black
Introduction to English Law, Philip James, Butterworth
Advertising Law Handbook, D Woolley, Business Books
Advertising Law, R G Lawson, Mcdonald & Evans
Law Made Simple, Colin Padfield, Heinemann

Other, more specialized textbooks on the law are normally available in leading UK bookshops. For Scottish law, and the laws of other European countries and the USA, you should consult the appropriate authorities and/or reference books.

Appendix 1

The Institute of Public Relations Code of Professional Conduct (October 2000)

INTRODUCTION

The Code of Professional Conduct has been drawn up by the Institute of Public Relations to set down standards which will, it is hoped, make for good relationships and reputable business dealing by public relations practitioners. There are other, internationally adopted, Codes of Conduct which have the support of the Institute.

The Code is binding on members of the Institute and is under constant review. The Code was approved by the Annual General Meeting in 2000. These Guidelines should be used in conjunction with other Guidelines and Recommended Practice Papers issued by the Institute from time to time. They are intended to assist members in interpreting the Code, but it must be emphasised that they cannot be all-embracing. Circumstances can vary and it is up to members to measure their conduct against the standards set by the Code of Conduct.

Complaints about breaches of the Code, which may come from any individual or organisation, including non-members, are investigated by the Institute's Professional Practices Committee which, if considered appropriate, may refer the matter to the Disciplinary Committee for action. The Code is in no way a substitute for the law of the land, and anyone seeking redress against a member should do so through the normal legal processes.

Arbitration over a dispute is not part of the function of the Professional Practices Committee, but the Committee can sometimes appoint three senior Fellows of the Institute to act as Arbitrators, provided all the parties connected with the dispute agree, in advance, to be bound by the outcome.

Nor does the Committee comment on the amount of fees charged by a member, since these are conditioned by many factors outside the Institute's control. Terms of business are usually negotiated in advance and should be adhered to.

Whilst the Committee will consider complaints about members from non-members, it is not usually able to consider complaints from members about non-members.

PRINCIPLES

1. Members of the Institute of Public Relations agree to:

    i.   Maintain the highest standards of professional endeavour, integrity, confidentiality, financial propriety and personal conduct;
    ii. Deal honestly and fairly in business with employers, employees, clients, fellow professionals, other professions and the public;
    iii. Respect the customs, practices and codes of clients, employers, colleagues, fellow professionals and other professions in all countries where they practise;
    iv. Take all reasonable care to ensure employment best practice including giving no cause for complaint of unfair discrimination on any grounds;
    v.   Work within the legal and regulatory frameworks affecting the practice of public relations in all countries where they practise;
    vi. Encourage professional training and development among members of the profession;
    vii. Respect and abide by this Code and related Notes of Guidance issued by the Institute of Public Relations and encourage others to do the same.

PRINCIPLES OF GOOD PRACTICE

2. Fundamental to good public relations practice are:

    Integrity

    ● Honest and responsible regard for the public interest;

- Checking the reliability and accuracy of information before dissemination;
- Never knowingly misleading clients, employers, employees, colleagues and fellow professionals about the nature of representation or what can be competently delivered and achieved;
- Supporting the IPR Principles by bringing to the attention of the IPR examples of malpractice and unprofessional conduct.

Competence

- Being aware of the limitations of professional competence: without limiting realistic scope for development, being willing to accept or delegate only that work for which practitioners are suitably skilled and experienced;
- Where appropriate, collaborating on projects to ensure the necessary skill base.

Transparency and conflicts of interest

- Disclosing to employers, clients or potential clients any financial interest in a supplier being recommended or engaged;
- Declaring conflicts of interest (or circumstances which may give rise to them) in writing to clients, potential clients and employers as soon as they arise;
- Ensuring that services provided are costed and accounted for in a manner that conforms to accepted business practice and ethics.

Confidentiality

- Safeguarding the confidences of present and former clients and employers;
- Being careful to avoid using confidential and 'insider' information to the disadvantage or prejudice of clients and employers, or to self-advantage of any kind;
- Not disclosing confidential information unless specific permission has been granted or the public interest is at stake or if required by law.

MAINTAINING PROFESSIONAL STANDARDS

3. IPR members are encouraged to spread awareness and pride in the public relations profession where practicable by, for example:

- Identifying and closing professional skills gaps through the Institute's Continuous Professional Development programme;
- Offering work experience to students interested in pursuing a career in public relations;
- Participating in the work of the Institute through the committee structure, special interest and vocational groups, training and networking events;
- Encouraging employees and colleagues to join and support the IPR;
- Displaying the IPR designatory letters on business stationery;

- Specifying a preference for IPR applicants for staff positions advertised;
- Evaluating the practice of public relations through use of the IPR Research & Evaluation Toolkit and other quality management and quality assurance systems (e.g. ISO standards); and constantly striving to improve the quality of business performance;
- Sharing information on good practice with members and, equally, referring perceived examples of poor practice to the Institute.

INTERPRETING THE CODE

4. In the interpretation of this code, the Laws of the Land shall apply.

Appendix 2

The law as it affects public relations practitioners

There are two sorts of law with which a public relations practitioner should be familiar: common law and statute law.

Common law concerns such things as contracts, civil wrongs or 'torts', ie ways in which an aggrieved party can seek compensation by suing in a civil court.

Statute law is that law created either by Act of Parliament or by regulation which makes offenders liable to prosecution, fine and/or imprisonment as a result of criminal proceedings between the Crown and the wrongdoer.

CONTRACTS

Contracts form one of the most common experiences in PR work. The law regarding contracts is complicated, and much has been written on the subject. There are many different types of contract, depending on the circumstances, ie those between a consultant and client, those for commissioning photography, leasing equipment, hiring exhibition contractors, etc. With any contract always remember:

- Read the small print before you sign it.
- Get your legal department to check it for you.

- Both sides must be quite clear as to the conditions and requirements.

Ideally a contract should be in writing, but it may be agreed by telephone or fax, for a photographic assignment, hotel or airline reservation, for instance. It can sometimes be verbal when hands are shaken as a sign of trust ('my word is my bond').

When discussing or corresponding about the possibility of new business contracts it is always safer to make it clear that any such correspondence or discussions are *'subject to contract'*. Otherwise situations can arise through misunderstanding, when a verbal contract is to be assumed without any formal document being drawn up. This can prove to be embarrassing, expensive and can lead to litigation.

What makes a contract?

Three components constitute a contract:

1. an offer;
2. an acceptance;
3. a consideration.

NB A one-sided bargain, such as a gift, is not a contract.

The offer
For an offer to be made there needs to be a definite intention to create a legal situation. If one side offers, then the other side must agree to accept that offer.

Acceptances and revised offers
An acceptance must be unconditional. However, if the acceptance of the offer is conditional and introduces new, different conditions, then it becomes a *revised offer* – which then needs an acceptance.

The considerations
The consideration is that both sides must give value to the other. One side supplies good or services, the other side pays for them. Both sides must surrender something of value to the other, although the fairness of the exchange is immaterial.

DEFAMATION

Defamation is defined as: 'The publication of a statement which exposes a person to hatred, ridicule or contempt or causes them to be shunned or avoided by right-thinking members of society generally.' The spoken form of defamation is slander; this is considered to be 'transitory' (ie it does not last). The written, and broadcast, form of defamation is libel.

Care must therefore always be taken by practitioners not to bring another person, organization, product or service into disrepute. Even if unintentional, the offence could result in an action for damages or an injunction being taken out to prevent further references being made.

To be slanderous or libellous a statement must be said to be:

- defamatory;
- false unless proved to the contrary;
- understood to refer to the plaintiff;
- made known to at least one person other than the plaintiff.

Examples of defamation

1. An article was written and about to be published widely in the UK about an internationally known personality. Details about that person were widely given in the article without permission first being obtained. The personality objected to the article and forbade its publication.

   Result – a High Court Injunction was obtained, seizing and destroying all copies of the publication containing the said article and all printing material concerned, including plates, proofs, film etc.
2. A photograph was published on the front cover of a well-known magazine showing a crowd with a ballooned comment purporting to come from an individual in that crowd.

   Result – that person sued for libel because the comment was false and could have been held to hold him in dispute.

PASSING OFF

Passing off is the misuse of a trade name, brand, or trade name of goods. It also covers the imitation of the 'get-up' or presentation of the goods concerned, which can include the container, the labelling and often the packaging.

However, if the products are in different areas of trade then no legal action can be taken. Examples of this are in the use of the word 'Colt': as in Colt beers, Colt cars and Colt guns; and in the title Amtrak: as in Amtrak the US rail company and Amtrak the British delivery company.

For a successful case to be brought under English law the plaintiff must show:

- that the trade name or 'get-up' of the offending goods is associated with his or her goods in the public mind;
- that the acts that are objected to have interfered with, or are calculated to interfere with, the conduct of business or sale of goods in the sense that there is or could be confusion in the public mind;
- the two products must be in a common area of trade.

> Fraudulent motive or public confusion does not have to be proved,
> only that it is likely to occur.

COMPETITIONS AND LOTTERIES

From time to time practitioners may get involved in this area either on behalf of clients or for their own organization. The following basic rules should be remembered:

- All competitions must contain an element of skill, otherwise they are liable to be illegal under the Betting, Gaming & Lotteries Act 1963 and subsequent amending lotteries acts.
- Correct answers in a competition must not be prejudged.
- Lucky draws are acceptable, but only for non-commercial circumstances.

If the competition is to be published in a newspaper the editor will want to check that:

- there are rules, and that there is adequate time for the submission of any rules;
- contestants are required to use their judgement;
- entries will be fairly and competently judged.

NB In a two-stage competition *both* parts must require a degree of skill.

Raffles

If you are intending to run a raffle at a local carnival, craft fair, charity dinner, or any similar type of function where tickets are sold to members of the public before the event, then the tickets must have the name and address of the organizer printed on them. It is best to check the by-laws in your area for local variations.

Offers

The offer of 'two for the price of one' found in some competitions may also be illegal. Again, it is worth checking with the terms and conditions of the Betting, Gaming & Lotteries Act.

Appendix 3

Model client agreement

AN AGREEMENT

Introduction

This agreement has been prepared to ensure that from the commencement of the Consultancy/Client relationship both parties fully understand their respective rights, duties and procedures.

The Consultancy will cooperate fully with the Client and take the initiative in offering advice and services. The Client agrees to assist the Consultancy in the performance of these duties by making available to the Consultancy all relevant information.

Consultancy status

The Consultancy acts in all its contracts as a principal at law.

Exclusivity

The Consultancy will not represent conflicting or competing interests without prior agreement by the Client who will advise the Consultancy in writing of any intention to engage additional internal or external public relations Consultancy services other than those already advised.

1. APPOINTMENT AND PROGRAMME

This Agreement confirms the appointment of

....

(hereinafter referred to as 'the Consultancy')

as Public Relations Consultants to

....

(hereinafter referred to as 'the Client')

to undertake such public relations programmes
as are detailed and which appear in the Consultancy's document

of .... (date)

2. COMMENCEMENT AND DURATION OF THE AGREEMENT

This appointment will commence on

....

and will continue in effect unless terminated under clause 10 of this Agreement.

3. FEES

The Consultancy's service fees exclusive of VAT and based on management, executive and administrative time in the United Kingdom will be calculated at the rate of

£ ....

These fees apply only to work carried out in the United Kingdom; they do not apply to international supervision of work performed abroad which will be subject to separate fee arrangements.

4. DISBURSEMENTS AND EXPENSES

The Consultancy fee shall be exclusive of the following disbursement and expense items relating to the agreed programme.

4.1. Disbursements

- Advertising, artwork and mechanical items (ie blocks, typesetting, films etc).
- Direct mail.
- Entertainment of media and other authorized individuals on the client's behalf.
- Exhibition and display material.
- Film production, design, artwork and printing.
- Market research.
- Media monitoring (radio, television and press).
- Newspaper and magazine subscriptions.
- Special events, meetings, conferences etc.
- Subsistence.

4.2. Expenses

- Messenger services.
- Postage and telephone charges.
- Photocopying, stationery and duplicating.
- Photography and the production of photographic prints.
- Telephone, fax, telex and cable charges.
- Travel expenses.

The Client agrees to pay immediately upon presentation any agreed interim invoices in respect of advance or instalment payments required to be made to suppliers.

The Consultancy reserves the right to request that it is put in funds by the Client whenever substantial advance payments or financial commitments are required on the Client's behalf.

5. PAYMENT TERMS

The Consultancy's fees are invoiced quarterly in advance. Disbursements and expenses are invoiced monthly in arrears. All fees, disbursements and expenses are payable within 30 days of the date on which they are rendered.

6. APPROVALS AND AUTHORITY

After obtaining general approval of campaign or project plans the Consultancy will submit to the client for specific approval all:

- draft press releases, articles, photographs and captions;
- copy, layouts, artwork and/or scripts;
- estimates of the costs of the various items of the programme.

Written or oral approval by the Client of the drafts, proofs and estimates will be taken by the Consultancy as authorization to proceed and such approval will be taken as authorization to enter into contracts with suppliers of goods and services on the basis of those estimates.

The Consultancy will take all reasonable steps to comply with any requests from the Client to amend or halt any plans or to reject or cancel any work in the process of preparation insofar as this is possible within the scope of its contractual obligations to its suppliers.

Any amendments or cancellations will be implemented by the Consultancy only on the understanding that the client will be responsible for any costs or expenses incurred prior to or as a result of the cancellation or amendment and which cannot be recovered by the Consultancy.

7. COPYRIGHT

The terms and conditions as set out in the Copyright, Design and Patents Act 1988 shall be deemed to apply.

7.1. Copyright

The Copyright in all artwork, copy and other work produced by the Consultancy rests initially with the Consultancy.

7.2. Assignment of Rights

On payment by the Client of the relevant Consultancy fees and charges in full, the copyright is automatically deemed to be assigned to the Client unless other arrangements are made.

8. CONFIDENTIAL INFORMATION

The Consultancy acknowledges a duty not to disclose without Client permission during or after its term of appointment any confidential information resulting from studies or surveys commissioned and paid for by the Client.

The Client in turn acknowledges the Consultancy's right to use as it sees fit any general intelligence regarding the Client's products or services which it has gained in the course of its appointment.

9. INSURANCE

9.1. Professional indemnity

The Client shall indemnify and keep indemnified the Consultancy from and against any and all proceedings, claims, damages, losses, expenses or liabilities which the Consultancy may incur or sustain as a direct or indirect result of, or in connection with, any information, representations, reports, data or material supplied, prepared or specifically approved, as described in paragraph 1 of Clause 6 of this Agreement, by the Client particularly in relation to proceedings under the Trade Descriptions Act 1968. Such material to include press releases, articles, copy, scripts, artwork and detailed plans or programmes.

9.2. Client's property

Any property or information made available by the Client to the Consultancy for the purposes of demonstration or publicity or for any other purpose arising from or in connection with this Agreement shall be and at all times remain the sole and entire risk of the Client and the Consultancy shall not be subject to any liability for it.

10. TERMINATION

The Client agrees to appoint the Consultancy for an initial period of .... After the initial period the appointment shall continue until either the Client or the Consultancy serves written notice to terminate the Agreement.

10.1. Period of notice

Three months will be given as a minimum unless separate agreements have been arrived at in writing between both parties.

10.2. Payment of fees, expenses, disbursements, etc

In the event of termination of this Agreement for whatever reason the Client will be responsible for all fees payable hereunder to the Consultancy, and costs and expenses and disbursements incurred by the Consultancy on behalf of the Client up to and including any notice period.

11. LIABILITY

Written or oral approval by Client of drafts, proofs and estimates will be taken by the Consultancy as authorization to proceed to publication and to enter into contracts with suppliers of goods and services on the basis of those estimates.

The Consultancy will not be liable for any delay in or omission of publication or transmission or any error in any press release, article, statement, notice or advertisement.

12. SUPPLEMENTARY

If, due to wars, strikes, industrial action short of strikes, lockouts, accidents, fire, blockade, import or export embargoes, ice obstructions, natural catastrophes or other obstacles over which the Consultancy has no control, the Consultancy fails to complete an assignment in the manner and within the time required by the terms of this Agreement the Consultancy shall not be held responsible for any loss or damage which may be incurred by the Client as a result of such failure.

For the purpose of the Unfair Contract Terms Act 1977 and any other relevant Acts each and every clause of this Agreement shall be read as defining the scope of, rather than attempting to exclude, liability.

Insofar as it is possible to exclude any provision of the aforementioned or any other relevant act, the Consultancy and Client agree to exclude any such provisions.

This Agreement shall be subject to English Law. Any transactions whatsoever of whatever nature carried out by the Consultancy including any services offered shall be on these terms and conditions alone. Any dealings with the Consultancy shall automatically be deemed to be acceptances of these terms and conditions whether or not any acknowledgement to this effect is signed.

The Headings to the paragraphs and sub-paragraphs in these terms shall not affect the construction of these terms.

13. STANDARDS AND CODES OF CONDUCT

The Consultancy undertakes to adhere to the Code of Practice as set down and revised from time to time by the Institute of Public Relations and all other codes of standards laid down by public relations and advertising industries to ensure all work undertaken by the Consultancy is at all times legal, decent, honest, ethical and truthful.

THIS AGREEMENT IS SIGNED:

FOR AND ON BEHALF
OF THE CONSULTANCY

FOR AND ON BEHALF
OF THE CLIENT

Signature ....

Signature ....

Position ....

Position ....

Date ....

Date ....

Appendix 4

Employment regulations

DEPARTMENT OF TRADE AND INDUSTRY

This has become a very complex area and one covered by a considerable amount of legislation, both UK and EU based. However, in essence, there are only two types of employment relationship: those of either contracts of service or contracts for services.

CONTRACTS OF SERVICE

A contract of service, also known as a contract of employment, is the legal relationship between an employer and employee, ie the normal contract for an employed person. It is used where the employer exercises a large degree of control continuously over an employee on a long-term basis.

Employers' liabilities

Under the terms of this type of contract the employer may be made liable under the laws for Torts, or wrong doings committed by his or her employees during the course of their employment. The law in this case also imposes a high standard of care on an employer with regard to health and safety of his or her employees, both under statute and common law.

Economic implications

Employees' income tax is deducted from their wages under the PAYE Scheme (Schedule E). Likewise, under the Social Security Act 1975 both employer and employee must contribute to the payment of Class 1 National Insurance contributions. An employee is then entitled to claim all available welfare benefits, eg unemployment, sickness, industrial injury etc.

Other statutory rights

The Employment Protection (Consolidation) Act of 1978 conferred a number of rights and benefits on an employed person, eg the right to written notice of details of employment (the contract of employment) within the first 13 weeks of employment, the right to receive certain minimum periods of notice of dismissal, the right to redundancy payment in appropriate circumstances, to protection against unfair dismissal, to be a member of a trade union and engage in union activities, and the right to protection against an employer's insolvency.

CONTRACTS FOR SERVICES

Used by self-employed people, contracts for services concern the carrying out of a specific task, or tasks, usually for a limited period or intermittently. They may not have as much control over standards of performance as a contract of service, although the terms of the contract may cover this. The task of distinguishing between the two types of contract has been left to the courts to decide in cases where there are doubts or problems. Any contract should tie in with IPR and/or PRCA codes of conduct.

Employers' liabilities

As a general rule, the employer is *not* liable for Torts committed by independent contractors during the course of their employment and has a lesser standard of care towards the contractor with regard to health and safety, both under common law and statute law.

Economic implications

A self-employed person is responsible for his or her own tax liability and pays tax under Schedule D on a preceding year basis. Under the Social Security Act 1975 the self-employed person is responsible for payment of lower rate Class 2 contributions. The self-employed person has no entitlement to certain welfare benefits, eg unemployment or industrial injury, but may claim others, eg sickness benefit.

Other statutory rights

The majority of the statutory rights under the Employment Protection (Consolidation) Act 1978 are not available for self-employed persons.

FURTHER INFORMATION

Further detailed information on particular different aspects of the law relating to employment and the related rules and regulations can be obtained through the Web on: www.dti.gov.uk/er/regs.htm. On this site you will find a great deal of information on regulatory guidance available, covering areas such as employment legislation, time off, maternity and other parental legislation, trade unions, Sunday trading and employment rights.

Appendix 5

Checklist of public relations assistance on the exhibition stand

Exhibitions: Record *all* visitors to the stand

Much of this information will also apply when running your own stand.

BEFORE THE EVENT

- Contact the **exhibition press office** – get all the detail you can. Who is opening the exhibition, when, where? Try and get the VIP and party on to your stand.
- Ensure you have a good selection of **promotional gifts**, that there are enough to last, and that they are appropriate to the event.

DURING THE EVENT

- Get your company's VIPs on the stand on **press/preview day**. Include the board members, or at least the chairman and CEO.
- Organize a **private press reception** on your stand.
- Check out the **media opportunities**. Find out what coverage is expected. Which TV networks and radio stations are covering the event?
- **Record all visitors** to the stand – have a visitors' book or equivalent.
- Check on any **press receptions** planned during the event. Where and when will they be held, and who will be there?
- Foster **media interest**. Find out about appropriate programmes/publications etc for the future.

AFTERWARDS

- The 'wash up':   It is most important to evaluate all the tangible results and look for any lessons learnt. What did the event achieve? Was it cost effective?
- Follow-up action: All visits and enquiries at your stand from potential clients/ customers and from the media must be followed up with a letter.
- Writeups: Freelance journalists may want to write up the exhibition, and your stand in particular, in feature articles after the event.

Appendix 6

Event and conference planning

CONFERENCE TRAVEL

Group travel arrangements

Some railway operating companies offer special group travel fares at reduced rates for parties of 10 or more people travelling together. This service can be incorporated into the conference booking for delegates. Enquiries should be made in the first instance to the customer services department of the railway company concerned, so that if this service is on offer, the details can be worked out and added to the relevant conference booking form.

Some numbers to ring are:

- GNER: 08457 225 333
- First Great Western: 08457 413 777
- Virgin Trains: 0870 010 4490
- Midland Mainline: 08457 125 678
- Scotrail: 08457 55 00 33

or you can visit them on their Web sites at:

- www.gner.uk
- www.firstgreatwestern.co.uk

- www.virgintrains.co.uk
- www.midlandmainline.com
- www.scotrail.co.uk

You can find out information on other rail companies, and the services that they offer, by contacting a firm called 'Q' Jump on 0870 000 7245 or 01142 537 642 or by e-mail on groups@qjump.co.uk.

For other information on national train fares and train times for destinations in the UK, The National Rail Enquiries can also help on 08457 484 950.

Appendix 7

Planning guidelines – events

Below are some bullet points for use when planning events generally which should be helpful to you when planning your own.

Before planning any event, first ask yourself the following questions:

- Is it newsworthy?
- Will it show the subject off well?
- Will it have the right atmosphere?
- Is it relevant?
- Is it appropriate?

If the answer to each of these is 'yes' then you can begin. In general terms, for planning purposes you need to:

- Get the budget allocated.
- Appoint a small planning group – probably no more than four people.
- Select the venue.
- Draw up an outline programme of events.
- Produce a timetable and detailed programme.
- Circulate these to all concerned in good time to allow for changes.
- Check the details.
- Have a wet weather programme (if applicable).

NB All work must be within budget limits.

Appendix 8

Planning guidelines – conferences

When planning a conference, as with events generally, you should first ask yourself the following questions:

- Why have it? – What will be achieved by staging it?
- Who is the keynote speaker? – Is there a personality attending?
- Who are the target audiences? – Who is it for?
- Is it a 'prestige' event? – Is it overseas or UK based? Is an exhibition included?

- What is the venue? – Hotel, stately home or conference centre?
- Will it be expensive? – How much is reasonable?
- How long is it to last? – A week, a weekend or only a day?
- When is it to be staged? – Will it clash with other major events?

A CHECKLIST FOR CONFERENCE PLANNING

Venue	Check availability beforehand. Don't forget time needed for rehearsals, mounting/dismantling the stand etc.
Facilities	Sound systems, A/V systems, TV and radio facilities. Have backup available. Rehearse with all equipment.

Book caterers	Liaise with whoever is in charge. Plan menus.
Programme of events	Circulate widely.
Brief Chair(s)	Also keynote speakers etc. Have copies of speeches available.
Audio-visual material	Check on copyright and equipment.
Train and rehearse	Presenters, speakers. Rehearse speeches etc.
Conference packs	Publications, folders, presentation transcripts, photographs.
Invitation and mailing lists	Compile a list in good time. Design, mail and follow up.
Programme	Send map of venue and general venue information to delegates.
Accommodation	Check on bookings/dietary requirements.
Travel arrangements	Entertainment/day trips/discounted arrangements for rail/airlines.
Mounting	Check on set design for stage, room layout, seating etc.
Translation service	May be needed.
Insurance and security	Liaise with venue organization.
Reception area	Registration of delegates, badges, information packs, timetable, delegate list, pens, pads.
Hire of equipment	Office equipment, fax machines, phones.

The above are some of the main points to remember, but the list is by no means exhaustive. There may well be other points particular to the event being planned that you should include.

Always make a checklist, otherwise you may forget something vital!

Further information that may help in the planning stages can be found in the *Conference & Incentive Travel* magazine. This monthly publication is aimed at those running conferences, organizing events or who plan incentives of some sort. For further information the publishers can be contacted by phone on 0208 267 4307 or by e-mail on cit@haynet.com.

Appendix 9

VIP visits

VIPs: Transport & Security

GENERAL PLANNING

Beforehand you need to know:

- the reason for the visit and its duration;
- the date and approximate timings for the visit;
- the locations to be visited (including your own);
- travel involved between locations, and timings;
- what security restrictions, if any, are involved;
- mode(s) of transport involved.

Having got the above general information, you can then plan the detailed timetable for your part of the visit within the overall programme. You need to know the following:

- How many will be in the party?
- What transport arrangements will be needed?
- Who they are to meet, where and when?
- When will they be received and by whom? What is the protocol?
- What presentations, if any, to be made on arrival?
- What locations are to be visited?
- What opportunities will there be to meet local people?
- Will there be 'walkabout' opportunities?
- What special arrangements need to be made for the media?
- Are VIP retiring room facilities required?
- Are refreshments to be offered? (Are there any special dietary requirements?)
- Are there any special requirements or requests from the VIP?

Appendix 10

Royal visits

Royal visits are comparatively rare but require meticulous planning and attention to detail. This type of visit varies enormously, depending on the category and status of the Royal concerned, and there are certain procedures to be followed. In the light of recent events, security for Royal visits has been considerably heightened and is now a major consideration to be taken into account when planning for such occasions.

WHO SHOULD BE INVITED?

You need to know which Royal personage would be most appropriate for your particular organization. Each one has their own special interests and support different charities and good causes. The offices of the Lord Lieutenancy for the county in which the visit is taking place can advise you on this and, more importantly, if and when he or she is likely to be available. (They will also advise you about visiting VIPs from overseas.) The offices will tell you to whom you should write in the first instance. Note that all correspondence relating to the visit should be copied to the Lieutenancy.

TIME TABLING

1. About six months prior to the proposed visit, write to the Private Secretary of the VIP concerned, setting out your request. If your invitation is accepted and put 'in the diary' then you can draw up your draft outline programme with

timings. You can probably make certain arrangements in advance (who will be involved, when and where).

2. Submit a draft programme to the Lieutenancy for their approval. This is usually required several months in advance.
3. Amend your draft programme as necessary. Resubmit for approval.
4. Finalize the programme and send it to the Lieutenancy. Allow for last minute changes to be made.
5. Submit lists of names of persons to be presented – this is for security vetting and for briefing purposes.
6. Liaise with police over final security arrangements.
7. Who is coming? Get details of the party accompanying the visitor (the Lord Lieutenant, ADC, Lady-in-waiting, Lord Mayor etc).
8. Presentations etc. Who is to present a bouquet (if appropriate)? Has it been ordered? Are there any special VIP/Royal preferences (or allergies)?
9. Alert the media if they are not already aware. Inform the COI and prepare news releases for distribution. (Remember to coordinate this through the Lieutenancy.)

The day before

Get confirmation of the time of arrival at your location, plus other details such as the mode of travel of the Royal party, size of police escort, etc. The police will usually sort things out for you.

On the day – security

There is usually a special Royal protection party, provided from the local police force, in addition to the bodyguard from the Royal protection squad. They can give you up-to-the-minute reports on the Royal progress and can often smooth the path with any recalcitrant media.

Appendix 11

Written reports

Tell what you are going to tell them, tell them and then tell them what you have told them.

A written report must always be:

- Acceptable – that is to say, well presented.
- Easily understood – use short sentences and paragraphs. Avoid jargon – or at least explain it.
- Objective – use the third person – never personalize a report.
- Factual but stylish – but see 'house styles' on page 75.
- Logical in the flow – where there are different kinds of information being presented make sure that they can all be easily and quickly located.
- Brief – be succinct – use short sentences and paragraphs.

A summary at the start can be helpful. You should also include a conclusion with any recommendations.

LAYOUT

When writing reports, it is useful to have a standard reference numbering system for all paragraphs and sub-paragraphs for ease of quick reference. Thus:

1.   Paragraph
   1.1   sub-paragraph
      1.1.1   sub-sub-paragraph and so on.

(But see also 'house styles' on page 75.) *Always* number the pages, and for statistics, costings etc use annex with their separate appendices if necessary.

Appendix 12

Agenda format

Agenda
For
Committee Meeting
to be held at
[wherever] at [time] on [date].
(always specify time, date & venue)

Apologies for absence.
These can be either in writing or given verbally.

1. Minutes of the previous meeting.
    Indicate here if they were previously circulated (specify date), or if they are to be tabled at the meeting.
2. Matters arising [and not dealt with elsewhere on the agenda].
3. Topic(s).
    The items to be discussed or dealt with at the meeting. They may be either 'tabled', 'spoken to' or attached to the agenda.
4. Any other business.
    Any items not already on the agenda but which need to be dealt with – or may be called for at the start by the chairman.
5. Date, time and venue of next meeting.

Agenda items should be numbered for ease of reference to papers/reports etc.

Appendix 13

Example of layout for an internal paper

Agenda Item...
Name of Committee
Short Title of Paper
Date of meeting

FULL TITLE OF PAPER

1. Summary

1.1. This section of the report should give a brief introduction to the topic and highlight the main reasons for it, any problems or the current situation generally, depending on the circumstances.

1.2. It should also give a précis of the arguments set out later in the report, and may recommend a course (or courses) of action to be taken, mention any cost implications and generally set the scene.

2.   Present position

2.1. Here the background is given to the present position as succinctly as possible. It should include details of the causes that have given rise to the present position.

3.   Possible solutions

3.1. It is often best to put forward several different possible solutions, or courses of action, that could be taken, with the arguments for and against each, together with an outline of costs involved.

3.2. Each course of action should have a headline followed by a brief explanatory paragraph.

4.   Preferred solution

The recommended course of action to be taken.

5.   Costings

The financial costs, any benefits arising and other details of relevant financial information. This will be helpful to any decision making. Any detailed breakdowns should be given in an appendix to the report.

6.   Conclusion

6.1. A summary of the action required, and the preferred solution.

6.2. Request for any approvals and any action to be taken.

Author of the report
Job title
Date ....

Appendix 14

Example of layout for minutes

Action
by

Present

The names, appointments and titles of those attending.

Apologies

Names etc of all those who have notified their absence.

1. Minutes of the last meeting

These should be signed and dated as a true record by the Chair. All headings thereafter to be numbered sequentially.*

2. Matters arising

2.1.   Unfinished business.
Any business recorded in the minutes that has not been dealt with, or is not on the agenda.

3. Agenda items

The main part of any minutes. The title of each item discussed should be the same as the relevant agenda item.
3.1.   Main headings.
These should be in capital letters.
3.2.   Sub-headings.
In lower case and emboldened.
3.3.   Names.
The names of individuals who raise matters should be recorded.
3.4.   Action to be taken.
Where any action is required the appropriate person's initials should be recorded in the right-hand column.

4. Any other business

Any item of business that the Chair or a member wishes to raise, but has not previously notified.

5. Date of next meeting

The date, time and venue for the next meeting.

*NB If a new committee has been set up and is meeting for the first time, all minutes should be numbered sequentially from 1; otherwise numbering is continued from the last minute. This can be very important for future reference.
   Refer to any specific 'house style' in use.

Appendix 15

Contingency planning for a crisis

BEFORE THE CRISIS

1. Identify – look at possible situations.
2. Plan – make simple contingency plans to cover different situations. They should include:
   - the crisis team (who are they?);
   - team leader and media spokespersons;
   - procedures for handling the media generally;
   - facilities available (accommodation, communications);
   - background information;
   - contact telephone numbers for key personnel.

Backing

- Ensure all plans are agreed, accepted and fully supported at the highest level.
- Copies of plans should be held by all concerned.
- Check and update plans at regular intervals.

Practice

Remember – practice makes perfect:

- Hold regular practices.
- Involve the emergency services.
- Hold 'mock' press briefings and conferences to familiarize and train media spokespersons.
- Ensure next-of-kin procedures are known.

DURING THE CRISIS

When it happens:

- Assemble team quickly – use the call-out system.
- Set up communications – activate all communications systems.
- Establish crisis centre – assemble key personnel. Organize staffing rosters.
- Press and Media packs – assemble background information.
- Press conference – prepare a separate room if possible.
- Log/Diary – start an incident log. Record all events by date/time.
- Synchronize timings – ensure all are on one master clock.
- Monitor the media – remember that deadlines vary between newspapers, TV and radio stations.
- Community relations – watch this aspect. It could be a vital factor in the credibility battle.
- Expert advice – have expert advice available to deflect the media in the early stages.
- Answers – prepare answers to (potentially damaging) questions from the media.
- Blame – do not apportion blame or speculate on this.
- Reporters – never go 'off the record' to the press.
- Compensation – do not reveal details of any compensation to the media. For insurance claims take advertising space in newspapers.
- Crank calls and letters – ignore all crank calls. Acknowledge all letters of support through the local press by taking advertisements.
- Next of kin – *always* confirm that the next of kin have been informed before releasing any names to the media.

THE PRESS CONFERENCE

'Tell it all, tell it fast and tell the truth.'

Do:

- Call the press conference as early as possible.
- Use it to brief and update media.
- Use a room where nothing else is going on.
- Organize it – if there is limited access arrange to 'pool' TV crews.
- Have as few spokespeople as possible.
- Have a chairperson – someone senior who is a good communicator.
- Ensure only bona-fide journalists attend.
- Have a 'minder' – use public relations personnel.
- Have specialist(s) available.
- Have other organizations involved present.
- Keep it simple – use visual aids.
- Have statement/news release and press packs ready.
- Allow questions at the end only.

Do not:

- Allow questions or interviews outside the press conference.
- Use body language that will distract.
- Just read out a prepared statement.
- Get side-tracked.
- Admit any form of liability.
- Specify amount or type of compensation.

AT THE FINISH

- Stand down – Stand down the crisis team/equipment, etc gradually as the situation eases. Staffing levels can be reduced inside the centre.
- Follow-up action – There will be considerable subsequent follow-up action needed, such as press conferences, news releases, articles, statements, and general correspondence.
- The inquiry – Make preparations for any subsequent inquiry that is to be held. Collect all logs, diaries, notes and other relevant written material that may be called as evidence. Keep all such material secure.
- Wash up and analysis – These are operational management lessons to be learnt from your experiences during the crisis. The outcome of your analysis may indicate revision of your contingency plans.

IN A CRISIS ALWAYS REMEMBER

Commitment	Management backing is vital.
Filing system	Have a good one for background information.
The team	Keep it small – key people only.
Credibility	Important to maintain it.
Clean up	Be prompt. It shows you are a responsible, caring organization.
Advertising	Useful and can help save time.
Local press	Can give you more aggravation than the nationals.
The local community	Don't forget them. Good relations are vital.
The secretariat	Sufficient staffing to handle the crisis.
Information provision	Everyone must have the same information at the same time – synchronize.
Training	Vital to ensure smooth running when it happens.

Index